Coming Up
by Neil D'Souza

D1633411

First performed at Watford Palace The

Cast (in alphabetical order)

Alan/Simon Fernandez	Neil D'Souza
Older Jacob/Ghalib/Vicar	Ravin J. Ganatra
Hanna/Cook/Mrs Pereira/Tiger	Clara Indrani
Young Jacob/Alice	Goldy Notay
Daniel/Father Alvarez	Mitesh Soni

All other parts played by members of the company.

Setting:
The action takes place in Mumbai in the present and Mangalore in the past.

Creative Team

Director	Brigid Larmour
Associate Director/Movement Director	Shona Morris
Designer	Rebecca Brower
Lighting Designer	Prema Mehta
Sound Designer/Composer	Arun Ghosh
Assistant Director	Scott Le Crass
Company Stage Manager	Maddie Baylis
Deputy Stage Manager	Maria Gibbons
Assistant Stage Manager	Emma Ryan
Wardrobe Supervisor	Mark Jones
Dialect Coach	Helen Ashton

With thanks to:
Ameet Chana, Jaz Deol, Aysha Kala, Shobu Kapoor, Nikesh Patel, Peter Singh, Divya Kasturi, Eli Rodrigues, Ethan Rodrigues and Lloyd Trott.

Writer's Note

Neil D'Souza

The title 'Coming Up' came out of a conversation I had with director Brigid Lamour in 2008. I was pitching ideas for new plays to her and had got through my top two without much joy – so started talking about a recent trip I had made to India to visit family, my first in 12 years; noting how different it was to the place I remembered from childhood holidays in the 1970s. I mentioned to her, in passing, that Indian guests visiting the UK in the 70s and 80s would often use the phrase 'India is coming up', in reference to the increasing variety of modern/western goods and services that were becoming available there. It is from here that this project began.

If in the 1970s 'Coming Up' was more an expression of India's aspirations, by the time I went in 2008, evidence of India's 'rise' was on open display in the malls, the upscale restaurants, the call centres. I noticed in my family, that this rapid rate of development had created a new middle class: the number of cars they owned, the foreign holidays they were planning, their expanding property portfolios. Still at the same time, the old trappings were there – most significantly the poverty, in all its manifestations be it homelessness or street children. I also asked myself, even if India's GDP had ballooned, what about social attitudes? Was culture so quick and easy to change? What were current day attitudes towards women?

Into this melting pot, went Alan, the protagonist, a British Asian, an 'English' Indian born here, brought up by parents born there, one of us, wanting to make a quick buck, while needing what we all need – love, understanding, and above all, connection.

And so the story began . . .

Directors' Note — Brigid Larmour and Shona Morris

Over the course of two decades, our collaborations have evolved into a movement based approach to theatre making, to reflect our commitment to the power of collaboration and the shared imagination of performers, creatives and audience. Movement and acting and the way we produce our plays are integrated.

Watford Palace Theatre produces theatre that is open hearted and socially aware and entertaining, and our work together sits within this philosophy.

Movement expresses the heart and the want of the character through action. It carries a story with power and immediacy, without high concept and high tech production styles. The actor is the heart of the work.

We work with our designers and collaborators to create a unified stage space that can serve as a playground to respond imaginatively to the text, in which we evolve the world of the play. The rehearsal process involves asking questions about place and character which we solve dynamically and physically. We have found that these solutions carry the action forward like a piece of music and we use the language of music and dynamics to make our work.

We like it when the audience sees movement and action as one thing, because it is the story we want them to experience.

We seek to place the actors in a magic space of possibilities which they change by the way they use the space, and in which they transform from character to character in full view, like turning on a sixpence. Music and lighting, therefore, don't direct the audience what to feel, as in a film, but take their place alongside the acting and movement to create the world of the play.

This world is created by the ensemble in front of you. We use the principles of Chorus/Ensemble based acting to change the space, instead of changing the set. This chorus work can create metaphor and meaning, a group of performers alive and in the moment to express a shared idea or collective response. So we enjoy taking you out of naturalism.

The world of the play that we create serves the text, the words and the ideas in the plays we are lucky enough to work on. We work closely with the writers to make sure their meaning is carried through the physical work we do. We believe that taking the text as a starting point, and finding the theatrical language it offers us without distorting its meaning, is a powerful way of approaching new text based writing. New writing is not always naturalistic, and we need varied approaches to explore the complexity of ideas it can (and should) provoke in audience and actor alike.

We celebrate the creativity of our writers, performers and collaborators: theatre is a shared conversation and we are proud to be part of it.

'No attempt is made to put the stage (and audience) in a trance' Brecht.

Cast Biographies (in alphabetical order)

Neil D'Souza Alan/Simon Fernandez

Neil trained at RADA and has since worked extensively in theatre, film, television and radio.

Theatre credits include: How To Hold Your Breath and Khandan (Royal Court); Drawing The Line (Hampstead); Much Ado About Nothing and Midnight's Children (RSC); Tintin (Watford Palace Theatre and West End); The Man Of Mode (National); Twelfth Night (West End); A Midsummer Night's Dream (Colchester, Mercury); Merchant Of Venice and The Honest Whore (Globe).

For Television Neil's work includes: EastEnders, Doctors, Hustle, Citizen Khan, Undercover, Holby City, Don't Take My Baby, Happiness, Back Up (BBC); Not Safe For Work, Friday Night Dinner, Raised by Wolves (Channel 4); Albert's Memorial, The Bill (ITV) and Amerikan Kannibal (Discovery).

Film work includes: Filth, Still Life, Closed Circuit, Wild Target, Another Me, My Sweet Home, Gate To Heaven and the lead role in Italian Movies (2012).

Radio includes: The Red Oleander, Goan Flame, Ask Mina, and the recurring drama Recent Events At Collington House (BBC Radio 4).

Ravin J. Ganatra Older Jacob/Ghalib/Vicar

Theatre credits include: The Deranged Marriage (Rifco and Watford Palace Theatre); Bombay Dreams (Really Useful); Passage to India (Shared Experience); Journey to the West, Revelations, Exodus, Nagwanti, The Bourgeois Gentelhomme (Tara Arts/Tour); The Mahabharata (National Tour); Natural World (Kali Theatre Co.); Hamlet, The Life of Galileo, The Winter's Tale, The Lion, the Witch & the Wardrobe (Library Theatre); Voices on the Wind, Aurangzebe (RNT Studio); The Wind in the Willows (Solent Peoples Theatre); Look Out Here Comes Trouble (Kaboodle); The Rammayana and Travesties.

Television credits include: The Infidel, Doctors, Coronation Street, In The Club, Hollyoaks, Rev, Torchwood, EastEnders, Nighty Night, Handle with Prayer, Waterloo Road, Britz, The Fugitives, Tom & Thomas, Entrapment, Prime Suspect, No Worries, Casualty, Holding On, The Brittas Empire, No Child of Mine and Circle of Deceit.

Radio credits include: Various productions for BBC Radio 4 and the World Service.

Clara Indrani Hanna/Cook/Mrs Pereira/Tiger

Clara trained at the London Academy of Music & Dramatic Art (LAMDA).

Recent theatre credits include The Deranged Marriage and Happy Birthday Sunita (Rifco and Watford Palace Theatre) where she made her professional stage debut.

Whilst at LAMDA she performed in many productions including A Gloriously Mucky Business, A Lie In The Mind, Cabaret, As You Like It, The Seagull and A Prayer for Owen Meany.

Clara's TV credits include: Led Astray (BBC); Hollyoaks (Lime Pictures) and Gates (Feelgood Fiction).

Goldy Notay Young Jacob/Alice

Theatre credits include: Happy Birthday Sunita (Rifco and Watford Palace Theatre); Speed (Kali); My Daughter's Trial (Kali); Tagore's Women (Kali); Handful of Henna (Sheffield Crucible); Zameen (Kali); The Deranged Marriage (Rifco and Watford Palace Theatre); Something about Simmy (Rifco); Blood Wedding (Theatre Passé Muraille/Toronto) and Romeo and Juliet (Waterspout/Bermuda).

Film credits include: The lead in It's A Wonderful Afterlife (Gurinder Chadha); My Own Country (Mira Nair); Sex and the City 2 (produced by Sarah Jessica Parker); London Dreams (Bollywood); Amar, Akbar, & Tony (Atul Malholtra) and Death Threat (Toronto Film Festival).

TV credits include: Silent Witness (BBC); Warehouse 13 (US Syfy); The Town (ITV Series); Holby City (BBC); The Bill (Talkback Thames); In a Heartbeat (Disney); Doctors (BBC) and Noddy (BBC).

Mitesh Soni Daniel/Father Alvarez

Mitesh trained at the Guildford School of Acting.

Theatre credits include: Banquo in Macbeth (Tara Arts – UK Tour); Paris/Prince in Romeo & Juliet (National Theatre); Second God in The Good Person of Sichuan (Colchester); Ali Baba in Arabian Nights (Manchester Library Theatre); Toalfish in This Place Means (Greenwich); Chulak in The Firework Maker's Daughter (Theatre by the Lake, Keswick); Billy in The Rise & Fall of Little Voice (Dukes, Lancaster); Tootles in Peter Pan (New Vic Stoke); Etash in Rafta Rafta (Bolton Octagon/New Vic Stoke); Mowgli in The Jungle Book (Birmingham Stage Company UK Tour); Beeny in Cloud Pictures (Polka Theatre); Naz in Mercury Fur (Goldsmiths); Simon in Lord of the Flies (Pilot Theatre UK tour); Luke in Meteorite (Hampstead Theatre); Betty/Cathy in Cloud 9 (Queen Mother Theatre) and Leonardo in Blood Wedding (Edinburgh Festival).

Film credits include: Rise of The Footsoldier 2, Syriana, Ghost of Life, Nine Lives London, Alpha Mayall and Lost Night.

Television credits include: Run, Threesome and The Canterbury Tales.

Awards: 2012 Manchester Theatre Award-Best Ensemble – Arabian Nights.

Creative Team Biographies

Neil D'Souza Writer

Neil has written for Theatre and Radio and has been commissioned to write for the TV.

Radio credits include: Four Beats To The Bar (Radio 4) and the long-running series Westway (BBC World Service). Neil's first play Small Miracle was produced by the Mercury Theatre, Colchester and subsequently transferred to the Tricycle Theatre, Kilburn. Television commissions include The Bollywoods – a sitcom for the BBC, and a comedy drama for Granada.

Brigid Larmour Director

Brigid is Artistic Director and Chief Executive of Watford Palace Theatre.

Productions directed for the Palace include: Jefferson's Garden by Timberlake Wertenbaker; Love Me Do (co-directed with Shona Morris) and Von Ribbentrop's Watch by Laurence Marks and Maurice Gran; Fourteen by Gurpreet Kaur Bhatti; Gary Owen's Perfect Match (part of the Ideal World season), We That Are Left and Mrs Reynolds and the Ruffian; Ronald Harwood's Equally Divided; Charlotte Keatley's Our Father and My Mother Said I Never Should; Alan Ayckbourn's Time of My Life and Absent Friends; Shakespeare's As You Like It; and pantomimes Mother Goose, Robin Hood and Sleeping Beauty (co-directed with Shona Morris), all by Andrew Pollard.

Brigid is a producer, director, dramaturg and teacher with experience in the subsidised and commercial theatre and television. From 1998 to 2006 she was Artistic Director of West End company Act Productions, and adviser to BBC4 Plays. From 1993 to 1998 she directed a series of promenade Shakespeares, Shakespeare Unplugged, for RNT Education.

From 1989 to 1994 she was Artistic Director of Contact Theatre, Manchester, commissioning the first British plays responding to the rave scene (Excess/XS), and the implications of virtual reality (Strange Attractors, a multimedia promenade production, by Manchester poet Kevin Fegan). She trained at the RSC, and as a studio director at Granada TV.

Shona Morris Movement Director/Associate Director

Shona trained at Ecole Jacques Lecoq.

Shona is currently Lead Movement Tutor at RADA and has just finished working at the Stratford Festival Theatre in Canada as Head of Movement.

Shona's recent productions for Watford Palace Theatre include: Jefferson's Garden (Movement Director); Sleeping Beauty by Andrew Pollard and the premier performance of Laurence Marks and Maurice Gran's play Love Me Do (both co-directed with Brigid Larmour).

Her recent work as Movement Director includes: Oedipus Rex, Hamlet, The Diary of Anne Frank, She Stoops to Conquer (2015), King John, A Midsummer Night's Dream, Hay Fever, Mother Courage, King Lear (2014), Romeo & Juliet, Blithe Spirit, Waiting for Godot, The Three Musketeers, Mary Stuart (2013), Peter Pan, Dangerous Liaisons, The Winter's Tale (2010) and The Birds, The Flies, Agamemnon, Electra, King Lear, Henry VIII (2004 – 2007) (Stratford Festival Theatre); Perfect Match, Override (2013), Our Father, My Mother Said, As You Like It, Lysistrata, The Dresser and An English Tragedy (2009 – 2012) (Watford Palace Theatre); The Snow Spider (2011) (Io Theatre); Atman (2010) (Finborough Theatre); Swine (2009) (National Theatre Studio); Nicholas Nickleby, Twelfth Night (2005 – 2008) (Chichester Festival Theatre); I Caught Crabs in Walberswick (2007) (Eastern Angles/Edinburgh Festival/Bush Theatre).

Shona's work as an actor includes: Chicken Soup with Barley (Nottingham Playhouse/ Tricycle Theatre); Augustine; Big Hysteria, Wax and Crossfire (Paines Plough).

Shona is a Creative Associate of Watford Palace.

Rebecca Brower Designer

Rebecca studied at Central School of Speech and Drama. Rebecca was the winner of The Stage Newspaper Design Award and The Equity Young Members Bursary Award in 2012. Rebecca was on the Design Team for the Opening and Closing Ceremonies for the London 2012 Olympic and Paralympic Games. Rebecca has also designed corporate events and dinners at The National Theatre.

Theatre Credits include: Treasure (Finborough Theatre); Genius Bar (UK Tour); Without Blinking (TestBed1, Goat and Monkey); Pal Joey (Mountview Academy of Arts); Beegu (Arts Depot); Dad Dancing (BAC); Struileag (Glasgow Green); Idylls of The King (Oxford Playhouse); Tender Loving Care (The New Theatre Royal, Portsmouth); Canterbury Tales (Watford Palace Theatre); Pursue Me (The Place); Jack and the Beanstalk (Southwalk Playhouse); This Child (The Bridewell Theatre); Lord of the Flies (Oxford Playhouse); Heartbreak Beautiful (Watford Palace Theatre); Hamlet (The Rose Theatre, Bankside. OffWest End Nomination, Best Set Design); I DO I DO (Riverside Studios); Hello Dolly (Watford Palace Theatre); Gypsy Bible (Opera North, National Tour) and A View From the Bridge (The Embassy Theatre).

Associate Credits include: Peter Pan (Regent's Park – Associate Designer); Bugsy Malone (The Lyric Hammersmith); The Great North Run Millionth Runner Ceremony (Newcastle, Outdoor Ceremony); The Roof (Fuel, The National Theatre UK tour) and Stuart a Life Backwards (High Tide, UK Tour).

Prema Mehta Lighting Designer

Prema graduated from The Guildhall School of Music and Drama.

She has designed the lighting for over one hundred drama and dance productions, including: Jefferson's Garden and Fourteen (Watford Palace Theatre); With A Little Bit Of Luck (Paines Plough, Latitude); Bells (The Mayor of London's outdoor festival, Showtime); Hercules (New Art Club on tour); Sufi Zen (Royal Festival Hall); The Great Extension (Theatre Royal Stratford East); The Electric Hills (Liverpool Everyman); Dhamaka (O2 Arena) and Maaya (Westminster Hall).

Prema recently lit for the launch of a new model in the A-list party area at Madame Tussauds. Prema is currently working with the National Theatre to deliver workshops and talks in lighting design.

Arun Ghosh Sound Designer/Composer

Arun Ghosh is a British-Asian clarinettist, composer and musical director. He has released three critically acclaimed albums, Northern Namaste, Primal Odyssey and A South Asian Suite, on camoci Records.

Other significant works in his repertoire include his re-score of feature-length animation The Adventures of Prince Achmed, contemporary dance work A Handful of Dust and programme symphony, Spitalfields Suite.

A key player on both UK and international jazz scenes, Arun is a renowned innovator of the Indo-Jazz style, and has appeared on the cover of Jazzwise and Jazz UK magazines in recent years. He was awarded 'Jazz Instrumentalist of the Year' at the 2014 Parliamentary Jazz Awards.

Arun is a prolific composer, working primarily in the world of theatre and dance. He has worked on over forty professional productions with companies including: Manchester Royal Exchange, Library Theatre, National Youth Theatre, Cardboard Citizens, Kadam, Akademi Dance, Tamasha and Kali Theatre. Coming Up is his second production for Watford Palace, having worked as composer and sound designer on Rifco's celebrated Deranged Marriage earlier this year.

Arun is an Associate Artist of The Albany Theatre and Spitalfields Music (2014), and recently completed his post as Musician in Residence of Wuhan, China in association with the British Council.

Scott Le Crass Assistant Director

Scott comes from Birmingham and trained as an actor at Arts Ed.

He was a director on the Birmingham Rep's first Foundry Programme.

Credits include: Director – Sid (Camden Fringe); Open House (Birmingham Rep and libraries tour); In A Better Place (Hotel Pelirocco/Brighton Fringe); The Bad Mood (Rich Mix/TROUPE Collective); Ode to Sid (One Festival/The Space); Diary of a Madman (Omnibus/Jack Studio); Boris Godonov, Marriage, Flight, Mandrake (Jack Studio); The Real Inspector Hound (Upstairs at the Gatehouse/ Camden Fringe); My Number 1 Favourite Lesbian by Tom Wells (Arcola/Outbox); La Mastication des Morts (Camden Peoples Theatre) and 35 Black Suits (Hidden Histories/Rep 100, Old Rep, Birmingham).

Assistant Director – The King's Speech (Chichester/Birmingham Rep/ UK Tour); A Christmas Carol (Birmingham Rep); Von Ribbentrop's Watch (Oxford Playhouse/Watford Palace); Kurt and Sid (Trafalgar Studios) and Henry VI, Part I (The Rose, Bankside).

Coming Up cast in rehearsals

Neil D'Souza

Mitesh Soni and Ravin J. Ganatra

Clara Indrani and Mitesh Soni

Goldy Notay

Clara Indrani, Neil D'Souza
and Ravin J. Ganatra

Goldy Notay, Neil D'Souza, Clara
Indrani and Ravin J. Ganatra

Photography by Richard Lakos

Watford Palace Theatre...

is a 21st century producing theatre, making new work across the art forms of theatre, dance, outdoor arts and digital, and developing audiences, artists and communities through exciting opportunities to participate.

Watford Palace Theatre commissions and produces plays from a range of new and established writers. Recent premieres include Jefferson's Garden by Timberlake Wertenbaker; Love Me Do by Laurence Marks and Maurice Gran; An Intervention by Mike Bartlett (in co-production with Paines Plough); Shiver by Daniel Kanaber; the Ideal World season of three new plays – Perfect Match by Gary Owen, Virgin by E.V.Crowe (in co-production with nabokov), Override by Stacey Gregg; Jumpers for Goalposts by Tom Wells (in co-production with Paines Plough and Hull Truck Theatre); Our Brother David by Anthony Clark; Our Father by Charlotte Keatley; and Family Business by Julian Mitchell.

Creative Associates are central to Watford Palace Theatre's vision these include Resident Companies Rifco Arts and Tiata Fahodzi; Mahogany Opera Group: Scamp Theatre; Kate Flatt; Shona Morris; Charlotte Keatley; Gary Owen; Alice Birch and Timberlake Wertenbaker.

Jefferson's Garden

Love Me Do

An Intervention

Shiver

Perfect Match

Jumpers for Goalposts

Friends
Support a local theatre with a national reputation

Our Friends receive (£45 per annum)
- Priority Information and Booking
- Discounted tickets (up to 20% on most performances)
- 20% discount on all beverages in our Cafe & Bar
- No card payment, postage or exchange fees

Our Good Friends receive (£90 per annum)
All of the above plus:
- 10% discount on hires of WPT Green Room Bar, Cafe & Hospitality Room
- Private backstage tours for up to 6 guests (normally £20)
- Acknowledgement in show programmes for WPT productions

Our Best & Business Friends receive (£500+ per annum)
- Private backstage tour for up to 12 guests (normally £30)
- Complimentary press night tickets plus drinks
- Opportunities to meet the cast of selected productions
- And more exclusive offers

With thanks to the Friends of Watford Palace Theatre:

Business Friends
Metro Printing
Warner Bros. Studios, Leavesden
Bushey Hall Garage

Best Friends
Bev and Paul Jullien and family
Deborah Lincoln
Frank and Helen Neale
Graham and Claire Buckland

Good Friends
Peter Freuchen
Paul Harris
Jarmo Kesanto
Steve and Lois Magraw
Chris and Mary Mitchell
M Parker
Linda Patel
Gary Townsend Vila
Norman and Mavis Tyrwhitt
PGC Young

Help Fund our Future

If Watford Palace Theatre and what it represents are important to you, please consider supporting us with a gift in your Will.

Whether you are a supporter of our work on stage, have an interest in engaging young people through theatre, or would simply like to support the Palace as a whole, we hope that you will consider remembering us with a gift in your Will.

Your most personal and lasting gift can be of any size; every donation helps and no amount is too small. By leaving a legacy you will be helping future audiences to discover the wonder of theatre and enjoy Watford Palace as you do today.

Watford Palace's charitable status may offer you the opportunity to reduce the tax due on your estate.

For further information please contact Lynne Misner, Development Manager, on 01923 257472 or alternatively email development@ watfordpalacetheatre.co.uk

Thank you for considering this special gesture.

Thank you to the members of the Green Room Donors Club for their generous support:

Gold Members
Dr Lewis Farrow
Mrs T Kcalcy
Mr Clive Payne
Mr John Perry
Mrs J Ryder
Mrs Adele Taylor
Mr Waterton
Mr Philip White

Silver Members
Mrs Margaret Ambrose
Mrs M Brown
Mrs Pamela Brown
Mrs L Cotes
Mrs Valerie Dutton
Mr Stephen Fordham
Mr D Gibney
Mr K Gooch
Mrs Pat Hiscock
Dr Eva Hnizdo
Mr Ian Laidlaw-Dickson
Ms Stella Merryweather
Mrs R Moore
Dr Margaret Murray
Ms Helen Payne
Mrs S Stalley
Mr Mark Watkin

COMING UP

Neil D'Souza

COMING UP

OBERON BOOKS
LONDON

WWW.OBERONBOOKS.COM

First published in 2015 by Oberon Books Ltd
521 Caledonian Road, London N7 9RH
Tel: +44 (0) 20 7607 3637 / Fax: +44 (0) 20 7607 3629
e-mail: info@oberonbooks.com
www.oberonbooks.com

A catalogue record for this book is available from the British
Library.

PB ISBN: 9781783199808
E ISBN: 9781783199815

Cover Design by Rebecca Pitt
Photography by Richard Lakos

Printed, bound and converted
by CPI Group (UK) Ltd, Croydon, CR0 4YY.

Visit www.oberonbooks.com to read more about all our books
and to buy them. You will also find features, author interviews and
news of any author events, and you can sign up for e-newsletters
so that you're always first to hear about our new releases.

For Martin and Sabina & Francis and Margaret
(English names for Indians through and through)

Characters

Notes on the text

My intention is that the play be performed by three to five actors, with virtuosity, regardless of age or gender.

Also that the use of different locations be achieved with maximum ingenuity/minimum fuss.

The characters, many of whose names sound English or Portuguese – are all Indian from Mangalore in South India.

This text went to press before the end of rehearsals so may differ from the final performance.

A Konkani song.

Two boys run on laughing and larking in Konkani, one of them sees something above and climbs up to reach it. He reaches and reaches.

The sound of an aeroplane landing.

ACT ONE

APARTMENT. MUMBAI. PRESENT

ALAN is at his Aunt's Apartment. It is clean and homely. She is in her eighties. Somewhere a TV is on softly – playing a Hindi comedy complete with slapstick noises.

ALAN: Well, it's been great to see you.

ALICE: Going?

ALAN: I have to Auntie.

ALICE: So soon?

ALAN: I have a meeting.

ALICE: Have something?

ALAN: I have a very boring meeting with clients

ALICE: I cooked.

ALAN: Next time.

ALICE: I haven't seen you in how long haven't I seen you in? twenty-five? thirty?

ALAN: thirty-three.

ALICE: thirty-three years. Next time I'll be up. Up!

A text arrives on ALAN's phone. He checks it.

The sender, HANNA, appears and speaks her text with great enthusiasm.

HANNA: 'When you want to succeed as bad as you want to breathe, then you'll be successful'

Beat.

ALICE: Why are you quiet?

ALAN: I'm not.

ALICE: Are you angry?

ALAN: I brought you a coffee machine.

ALICE: The thing?

ALAN: Nespresso. Top of the range.

ALICE: Why did you bring it idiot?

ALAN: It's a gift.

ALICE: Who asked you to bring gifts?

ALAN: I wanted to get you something. You put a capsule in / water in …

ALICE: Do you like coffee?

ALAN: Do I like coffee? Do you like coffee is the question.

ALICE: Do I like coffee? Do I like coffee … ?

Long pause.

ALICE: I like coffee.

ALAN: Great.

ALICE: But, your Daddy always used to bring me edam.

ALAN: Edam?

ALICE: Because Edam we don't get. Wait. *(She wanders off into the next room)*

ALAN: Auntie! I have to go.

But, she's out of the room. ALAN sits on the sofa. He feels the sofa, remembers it. DANIEL runs in (aged seven) he points a finger-gun at ALAN (aged eight).

1977.

DANIEL: *(Sings.)* Tantanaa!

ALAN dives for cover as DANIEL shoots.

DANIEL: I'm agent 116. You're a goonda.

ALAN: No, I'm agent 116!

DANIEL: *(Jumping on ALAN.)* No, I'm agent 116 and you're the Bad Boss.

ALAN: No, I want to be agent 116!

DANIEL: No, I'm agent 116. *(Mock hitting him.)* Piow! Piow! Agent 116 defeats the Bad Boss!

ALAN: No, I'm James Bond!

DANIEL: No, I want to be James Bond!

ALAN: *(Wrestling him to the ground.)* No, I'm James Bond. James Bond defeats Agent 116! *(Sings.)* Tantanaaa!

DANIEL: No, James Bond is defeated by Agent 116! (*Sings.*) Tantanaaa!

ALAN: No, I am the bionic man.

DANIEL: What?

ALAN: When I press my bionic watch, I have bionic powers.

ALAN presses his watch, makes the 'bionic sound' and turns DANIEL over.

ALAN: The bionic man defeats Agent 116!

DANIEL: No!

ALAN: The bionic man wins!

ALICE comes back into the room.

ALICE: You phoned Daniel?

ALAN: Haven't had time.

ALICE: I remember you as small boys running around. You got ill – puking and shitting – remember we had to take you to hospital?

ALAN: How is Daniel?

ALICE: Unmarried.

ALAN: He's in business, isn't he?

ALICE: Was. Now he's working for NGO.

ALAN: NGO?

ALICE: Charity.

ALAN: Oh.

ALICE: Speak to him. Find him a wife.

ALAN: Me?

ALICE: You are settled, aren't you?

ALAN: Yes.

ALICE: Your wife's name is?

ALAN: Anya.

ALICE: She's white?

ALAN: Yes.

ALICE: A dancer, isn't she?

ALAN: Used to be. Yoga teacher.

ALICE: Indian yoga?

ALAN: Hot yoga. They heat the room up Auntie.

ALICE: Why?

ALAN: To make the body more flexible.

ALICE: Are white people supposed to bend?

Beat.

ALICE: Next time bring her.

ALAN: I will. I will …

ALICE: Eat biscuits.

ALAN: I don't want biscuits.

ALICE: Eat something

ALAN: My driver's outside.

ALICE: Wait …

ALAN: Auntie I have to run!

But, she has wandered off …

He gets up and wanders over to the Crucifix. He kneels down before it.

DANIEL aged seven comes in and kneels down next to ALAN, now aged eight.

DANIEL /ALAN: Our Father
                            Who art in heaven
                            Hallowed be thy name.

ALAN gets up.

DANIEL: What are you doing?

ALAN: I'm bored.

DANIEL: Kneel and pray!

ALAN: No one's watching us.

DANIEL: God is watching us.

ALAN: I don't believe in God.

DANIEL: Junglee! Saying that in front of Our Lord.

ALAN: It was your fault anyway.

DANIEL: My fault? Who threw the cushion?!

ALAN: Who put their hands in the air like a poof!

DANIEL: A what?

ALAN: Gay boy! Poof!

DANIEL: What is poof?

ALAN: You want to know? You really want to know?

DANIEL: Yes.

ALAN: You are!

DANIEL: I'll give one thump!

ALAN: I'll thump you – Poof!

They fight.

DANIEL: Or I'll call your Daddy. Shall I call your Daddy? Uncle! Uncle!

ALAN: *(Panic.)* Shut up! Shut up!

He stands.

PRESENT

ALICE comes back in the room. She hums 'How Great Thou Art'

ALAN: I know that song…

ALICE: It's a hymn idiot. Do you pray?

ALAN: We had to kneel and pray in front of that.

ALICE: Yaw'l were devils.

ALAN: In the old place.

ALICE: You remember the old place?

ALAN: Yes.

ALICE: We moved here in 93. Thanks to your Daddy. He gave the money. Mind you he came and lived here at the end – nearly two years.

Beat.

ALICE: Why you never came?

ALAN: We didn't speak.

ALICE: We called you so many times.

ALAN: I'm very busy

ALICE: You were in Bombay only

ALAN: Working. I have a job. I have a very busy job

ALICE: Even for his funeral?

ALAN is silent.

ALAN: After Mum died we didn't speak. Fifteen years. Separate ways. No biggie. It's fine. We moved on. We were never on the same page.

ALICE: That's it!

She goes over to the shelf, takes a book.

ALICE: That's what I looking for!

She presents it to him.

ALAN: What?

ALICE: That's my gift to you.

ALAN examines the book.

ALAN: *(Reading Title.)* 'Coming up'?

ALICE: Those last two years he sat in that room writing.

ALAN: Dad wrote this?

ALICE: Day and night, writing.

ALAN: Dad wrote this?

ALICE: Read it.

ALAN: I don't read.

ALICE: Read it. Then on Wednesday come. Daniel will be here also.

ALICE leaves the room.

ALAN examines the book. He opens it.

JACOB – his late father – appears in the room, about seventy years old.

OLDER JACOB: 'Dearest Alan, it is now more then sixty years since I and my brother Albert, made our daily trek to the village school – two little boys larking in the jungle, larking, laughing, running for dear life when we smelt tiger's piss in the trees. Then one day, I saw it - the most beautiful mango in the tree, I reached up for it, I reached, I reached …

A roar.

Faster we ran than our little legs could run. Albert fell and hurt his foot. I went back for him, but the beast was nowhere to be seen. How perturbed I was! How disturbed! For I had to carry Albert two miles home.

Yet that was an auspicious day for me, a pivotal point. For the next, instead of making the daily, trek alone, I was sent to mass at St Joseph's Church, Pezar.'

ALAN closes the book.

THE CAR. MUMBAI. PRESENT

Aircon. Tinted glass.

ALAN is on an earpiece. Somewhere near there is a Ganapathy Parade.

ALAN: *(On Phone.)* … I dunno. I haven't read it yet … She gave me tea and biscuits … I don't know what biscuits. Indian biscuits …

DRIVER: Arre! Traffic.

ALAN: *(Back into phone.)* She'd cooked. I didn't eat it … Anyway it's done …

DRIVER: Too much traffic.

ALAN: You okay?

DRIVER: So, much traffic sake of Ganapathy.

ALAN: Okay. Okay. Bye. *He hangs up (To the DRIVER.)* What's your name?

DRIVER: Ghalib, Sir.

ALAN: What?

DRIVER: Ghalib.

ALAN: Right … Rule one: no talking when I'm on the phone, okay?

DRIVER: Okay Sir. Sorry, Sir.

ALAN: What happened to the other driver?

DRIVER: He start his own business Sir. Driving only.

A Ganapathy parade is outside.

ALAN: What's this?

The Parade comes near the car.

DRIVER: This Ganapathy, Sir. Birthday of Ganesh.

ALAN: Who?

The Parade passes through them.

ALAN: How can they dance in this heat?

The Parade passes.

DRIVER: Sir, I driver forty-three years to be of service my number one responsibility.

ALAN opens the book.

PAROCHIAL HOUSE. MANGALORE 1938

OLDER JACOB: 1938. The Vicar Forane in harness at Pezar parish was the Most Reverend Fr. Xavier Mendonza – a veritable deity in our midst. So imagine the honour, when at the end of mass, he invited me into the parochial house for a chat.

PAROCHIAL HOUSE

The VICAR sits staring at the eight year old JACOB.

Long Silence – except for the ticking clock

OLDER JACOB: Conversation was somewhat stilted, so I passed the time by observing a fly that was buzzing round his head. Then something happened, lightning struck!

VICAR: What is your name?

JACOB: Jacob, your Grace.

VICAR: What caste are you?

OLDER JACOB: Now this was a conundrum, Alan because in theory we were all God's Children, the Hindu caste system having no place in our Christian faith, in parctise, however …

JACOB: We are Sudirs, Sir.

VICAR: Farm workers.

JACOB: Yes.

VICAR: Do you pray?

JACOB: Yes, your Grace.

OLDER JACOB: It is now that lightning strikes.

VICAR: Every day?

JACOB: Yes, your Grace.

OLDER JACOB: Sorry it is now that lightning strikes.

A knock at the door. COOK enters, a woman, thrity-five with well-oiled hair.

COOK: Your Grace.

VICAR: What is it?

COOK: The altar boy is unwell.

VICAR: What is the matter?

COOK: He has been struck by lightning.

The VICAR closes his eyes, crosses himself. The COOK follows suit …

JACOB: Your Grace

OLDER JACOB: Sorry it is now that lightning strikes.

JACOB: If you are looking for a new altar boy …

Awkward silence the clock stops, everyone looks at JACOB.

VICAR: You know the Latin Mass?

JACOB: Yes, your Grace.

OLDER JACOB: This was untrue.

VICAR: But, altar boys must live here in the parochial house.

JACOB: To serve God is the aim of my life.

OLDER JACOB: Also untrue, but let's leave this here and for a brief moment, consider lightning. For in an average human life of threescore and ten, of doubt and indecision, how often will it strike?

RESTAURANT. MUMBAI. PRESENT

High-class restaurant. Members's Enclosure. HANNA at a table. Darkly lit.

A HOSTESS hovers.

HANNA: Hey!

ALAN: Don't get up.

They kiss. It is a bit awkward.

HANNA: How was your flight?

ALAN: It landed.

The HOSTESS approaches.

HOSTESS: Can I get you something to drink, Sir? We have an excellent Bollinger in stock.

ALAN: Two glasses.

The hostess smiles as she leaves.

HANNA: *(Whispers.)* What's a Bollinger?

ALAN: Surprise.

HANNA: What for Al?

ALAN: To thank you for all your work.

HANNA: Are you sacking me?

ALAN: What?

HANNA: I'm joking / It's a joke

ALAN: Oh …

HANNA: It's in my job description Al – work

ALAN: You like this place?

HANNA: It's romantic like the movies. Makes me want to sing

ALAN: Don't! *(Off her look.)* I don't like Bollywood.

HANNA: I don't like her. She was looking at my shirt.

ALAN: Relax.

HANNA: I am relaxed. Actually, I was thinking about this twenty-eight day returns policy

ALAN: Right

HANNA: I know customers like it and all, but people are routinely ordering goods and returning them soiled

ALAN: Do we have to talk about this?

HANNA: What do you want to talk about?

ALAN: I don't know.

HANNA: London.

ALAN: Have you seen the lobsters in the tank?

She looks.

ALAN: You have to choose one. Look.

They wander over to the tank.

HANNA: To eat?

ALAN: No, to take home as pets.

HANNA: Maybe they're thinking which one of us is next?

ALAN: You're thinking. You're overthinking. You're going to hurt yourself thinking.

The HOSTESS arrives with champagne and glasses.

HOSTESS: Your champagne Sir.

ALAN: Thank you.

The HOSTESS pours the drinks smiling and leaves.

HANNA: She is laughing at me.

ALAN: She isn't.

HANNA: She's smiling Al.

ALAN: She's paid to smile. Jesus! If you're going to be like this /

HANNA: You'll put me over your knee?

Beat.

HANNA: So, tell me

ALAN: What?

HANNA: About London – any news?

ALAN: It's fine. You're fine.

HANNA: Really?

ALAN: Yes.

Beat.

HANNA: Is my shirt really okay?

ALAN: Yes.

HANNA: I'm a lobster Al. Have you decided which one you want?

He holds her hand.

PAROCHIAL HOUSE. KITCHEN. 1938

OLDER JACOB: Thus it was my school career began in less than auspicious circumstances, scrubbing latrines to be exact – the Vicar decreeing I could attend classes only if my chores were done, the cook and her husband, the dried fish seller, seeing to it that moment never came.

JACOB scrubs the floor of the latrine. The COOK and the dried FISH SELLER look on.

COOK: Doesn't say much, but he is proud.

DRIED FISH SELLER: Bad.

COOK: Think you're better than this, do you?

JACOB scrubs.

DRIED FISH SELLER: Very bad.

JACOB: I'm hungry.

COOK: We're all hungry.

JACOB: I had no dinner, no breakfast …

COOK: You think I had breakfast?

JACOB: You did. You had idli sambar. I saw you.

COOK: I slave for this place.

Beat.

COOK: So, you're hungry?

JACOB keeps scrubbing.

COOK: You want idli sambar?

JACOB stops and looks up.

COOK: Shall I give?

DRIED FISH SELLER: Give! Give!

COOK: Come.

JACOB hesitates.

COOK: Come – bring the bucket!

JACOB approaches. The DRIED FISH SELLER empties the bucket over JACOB's head.

The COOK and the DRIED FISH SELLER laugh.

OLDER JACOB: At night cooped up in my cubby hole,
I attempted to memorise the Latin mass: Imagine, if you
will, the dingiest nook, under stairs, a cupboard where
provisions are stored – spices, oils, dried fish, mice, lice
centipedes of all varieties … while shut away a little boy
crams Latin in the dying light of a kerosene lamp

JACOB: Pater Noster, qui es in caelis,
                     Sanctificetur nomen tuum.
                     Adveniat regnum … *(falling asleep.)*

COOK: *(Now drunk, banging on the door.)* Wake up!

JACOB: I'm asleep.

COOK: Wake up or I'll put you in eternal sleep.

JACOB crawls out. Outside the moustachioed DRIED FISH SELLER smiles his lascivious smile.

DRIED FISH SELLER: Sleeping?

JACOB: Yes.

DRIED FISH SELLER: Of what were you dreaming?

JACOB: *(Defensive.)* Nothing. No one.

DRIED FISH SELLER: Girl no one or boy no one?

DRIED FISH SELLER has a very dirty laugh

OLDER JACOB: The cook came to get coconut oil for her hair.

COOK: Now sleep!

JACOB: *(From behind the door.)* I'm awake.

COOK: Then learn your Latin prayers!

JACOB: *(In the dark behind closed doors.)*
                     Pater Noster, qui es in caelis
                     Sanctificetur nomen tuum.
                     Adveniat regnum …

It is now day and JACOB is reciting the prayers in front of the VICAR.

VICAR'S STUDY

JACOB: Fiat voluntas tua,
                         Sicut in caelo, et in terra.
                         Panem nostrum quotidianum da nobis…
                         Er…Panem nostrum quotidianum da nobis…

VICAR: So, you know the Latin mass, do you?

The VICAR lifts JACOB by his ears violently, mercilessly.

JACOB: *(Lifted by the ears JACOB squeals the prayer at speed.)*
                         Panem nostrum quotidianum da nobis …
                         Et dimitte nobis debita nostra,
                         Sicut et nos dimittimus debitoribus nostris.
                         Et ne nos inducas in tentationem,
                         Sed libera nos a malo.
                         Amen.

The VICAR puts JACOB down, who nurses his bleeding ears.

VICAR: Good boy. *(Patting JACOB's head.)* Go walk by the river

Still nursing his ears, JACOB dawdles by the river …

A vision appears: A Lady in a veil, celestial light streaming. From somewhere Schubert's 'Ave Maria' can be heard. JACOB falls to his knees.

JACOB: Oh blessed Virgin! Mercy Mother! Is it you?

The woman takes off her veil. The music stops.

OLDER JACOB: No, it was Mrs Pereira – the English teacher.

As JACOB sits there, an amber light can be seen coming through the trees. It gets more intense throughout the next speech.

OLDER JACOB: But, mercy is the lesson here and the moral bankruptcy of those who attempt to beat knowledge into pupils. To what end? In my own life, with my own offspring I have sought another path of reason and patience – for though the physical scars of such indiscriminate violence heal in time, the psychological scars forever remain

ALAN throws the book against the wall.

HANNA emerges out of the amber light and comes into the hotel room …

HOTEL ROOM. MUMBAI.

Soft light, mod cons, air con.

HANNA: Al?

> *ALAN is silent.*

> What happened?

> *ALAN is silent.*

> Can't sleep?

> *ALAN is silent.*

> What's the book?

ALAN: Nothing

HANNA: *(Going over to the book.)* 'Coming up'

ALAN: Leave it

HANNA: Good book?

ALAN: Leave it I said.

HANNA: Are you upset?

ALAN: No.

HANNA: Come to bed.

ALAN: Don't you have an early call?

HANNA: Since when did you care about that?

ALAN: You said you had an early call.

> *Beat.*

HANNA: Not this again. You want me. You can't stop looking at me and then when you've got me … what is it, British humour?

> *She starts to get her things together.*

HANNA: I'm not doing this. Business is simple. This is not simple: worrying when you go away, what it means when you don't put a smiley on your SMS, when you put a small kiss instead of a big kiss /

ALAN: You're overthinking.

He picks up the book.

HANNA: What are you thinking?

Beat.

I have worked so hard to get here, to earn the respect of my team. I can't be doing this with you in the evenings and seeing them in the office in the mornings / in the training room …

ALAN: You won't have to.

HANNA: What are you talking /

ALAN: We're relocating. Manila. It's business.

Beat.

HANNA: You lied?

ALAN: When we moved out here you think people in the UK didn't / lose their jobs?

HANNA: You lied.

ALAN: We'll give you a generous pay out.

HANNA: No.

ALAN: Hanna /

HANNA: No

She leaves.

HANNA: We're just Indians to you aren't we Al? Cheap fucking Indians.

MANGALORE. SCHOOL CHOIR
_____

FR. ALVARES conducts the choir who sing. (It could be JACOB's Solo.)

> *HYMN.*
>
> O Lord my God,
> When I in awesome wonder
> Consider all
> The works Thy Hand hath made
> I see the stars,
> I hear the mighty thunder,

>   Thy pow'r throughout
>   The universe displayed;

OLDER JACOB: *(Over the above.)* As altar boy I was allowed to attend choir parctise. Our Master was one Fr. Alvares – an inspirational pastor. I remember him now: his kind eyes, his voice steeped in sadness.

>   Then sings my soul
>   My Saviour God to thee
>   How Great Thou art
>   How Great Thou art

OLDER JACOB: *(Over the above.)* Some said he could perform miracles, others that the only miracle was how he managed to stay standing after his daily dose of toddy, usually taken at lunch.

>   Then sings my soul

FR. ALVARES: Boys, that top note – flat. Again.

CHOIR: *(Sings.)*

>   Then sings my soul

FR. ALVARES: *(Sings.)*

>   Then sings my soul

CHOIR: *(Sings.)*

>   Then sings my soul

FR. ALVARES: You must believe, even if you have doubts, even if you sense the mire, *(He now points to the statue of the crucified Christ.)* for see how he believed, what they did to him – his hands, his feet – such is the fate of a good man in a sinful world *(FR. ALVARES is moved.)* Inspire yourselves boys and sing!

OLDER JACOB: In the afternoons I would be sent to water the Vicar's special coconut trees, where wondrous words would waft to me on the wind. From whence would these wondrous words waft?

MRS PEREIRA recites Wordsworth with the pupils, her big boobs perfectly poised.

CLASS: I wondered Lonely as a cloud

        That floats on high o'er vales and hills

        When all at once I saw a crowd,

        A host, of golden daffodils;

OLDER JACOB: It was the Virgin.

MRS PEREIRA: The poet talks of walking beside a lake only to be inspired by the sight of yellow daffodils, but we have beauty here in India too. Last time I asked you to compose a poem to the beauty of nature around you. Who has composed the poem?

The class is dumbfounded by her breasts.

MRS PEREIRA: Simon?

Stunned SIMON cannot answer.

MRS PEREIRA: Simon!

SIMON: Ma'am

MRS PEREIRA: Have you composed the poem?

SIMON: Yes, Ma'am.

MRS PEREIRA: Recite it please.

SIMON: Mangoes

 Juicy mangoes in the trees

 Swaying gently in the breeze

 When I see you I think please

 Please please please please please

MRS PEREIRA: Is that it?

SIMON: Yes, Ma'am.

MRS PEREIRA: It is rather short. Who else? Salvador – what is your poem called?

SALVADOR: Tender Coconuts.

HYMN REPRISE (CHORUS IN HARMONY.)

> Oh juicy mangoes
> Swaying in the breeze
> How Great Thou art!
> How Great Thou art!
> Oh juicy mangoes
> Please, please, please, please, please,
> How Great Thou art!
> How Great Thou art!
>
> *A knock at the door.*

HOTEL ROOM. MUMBAI. PRESENT

A loud banging at the door.

It is GHALIB.

ALAN: What?

GHALIB: I want speak Sir …

ALAN: It's 3 a.m.

> *Beat.*

GHALIB: Good room Sir. Pukka room. Company pay?

ALAN: What?

GHALIB: Sir, in London, where you live?

ALAN: Why?

GHALIB: Sir, I have idea. Business idea – big, big, very big.

ALAN: Are you drunk?

GHALIB: No Sir. I not drink. Musselman.

ALAN: So, what are you talking about?

GHALIB: That I cannot say.

ALAN: So, you came up here …?

GHALIB: Yes, Sir.

ALAN: Why did you come up here?

GHALIB: Yes Sir.

ALAN: WHY ARE YOU HERE?

GHALIB: Business …

ALAN: Piss off!

GHALIB: Sorry.

ALAN: I'll be having words with your boss.

GHALIB: Sorry. Sorry.

> *GHALIB is leaving.*

GHALIB: Sir, I also thinking about Ms Hanna, Sir.

ALAN: What about her?

GHALIB: I saw her leaving hotel Sir.

ALAN: She was collecting some papers for our meeting.

GHALIB: She upset Sir. Crying.

ALAN: Have you been spying on us?

GHALIB: I know she Sir. I her Father good friend.

> *Beat.*

GHALIB: She good person Sir.

ALAN: I know.

GHALIB: I know you know, Sir. You, she good friends. She thinking most highly of you.

ALAN: Are all Indians crazy or it just the women?

> *GHALIB waggles his head.*

ALAN: Is that a yes or a no?

> *GHALIB waggles his head.*

ALAN: Or is it just fucking complicated like life?

> *Beat.*

GHALIB: Life like that Sir, but in your heart, you know.

> *Beat.*

GHALIB: *(Going.)* Good night.

ALAN: Hang on! *(Handing him some money out of his wallet.)* Get yourself a KFC.

GHALIB: KFC?

GHALIB looks confused.

ALAN: Treat yourself. Something to eat.

GHALIB: No.

ALAN: Take it. Take it.

GHALIB takes the money.

ALAN: And keep this between ourselves okay?

GHALIB waggles his head and leaves.

GHALIB: Sir I driver forty-three years to be of service my number one responsibility.

He goes.

THE SCHOOL COMPOUND, MANGALORE, 1939

OLDER JACOB: Our annual sports day was like that of a British Public school without shoes. That year most of the boys had been struck down by fever (quite possibly on account of the way the cook made me chop vegetables after cleaning the latrines.) But, owing to shortage of runners, I was told to join the sprint. It was just I and Simon Fernandes.

OLDER JACOB: Go!

SIMON FERNANDES easily takes the lead.

OLDER JACOB: Simon Fernandes was high caste. King in studies. King in sports. His father owned a tile factory.

JACOB struggles to catch up with SIMON FERNANDES, but SIMON easily maintains his lead.

SIMON FERNANDES: *(Chanting to LITTLE JACOB.)* Your Father is a beggar! Your Father is a beggar!

OLDER JACOB: I was losing heart, when I suddenly thought of my daily trek through the jungle, of my brother and I running for dear life when we smelled the tiger's piss on the trees. I just thought of that tiger's piss smell.

JACOB now speeds up until he is neck and neck with SIMON FERNANDES. Faster still, JACOB now edges ahead.

SIMON FERNANDES: *(Chanting desperately now.)* My Father owns a tile factory! My Father owns a tile factory!

SIMON now edges ahead.

An imaginary TIGER is now chasing JACOB as he passes SIMON FERNANDES, clearly beating him to the finish line.

JACOB: I won, I won!

VICAR: I declare Simon Fernandes the winner.

JACOB: I won! I won!

VICAR: I declare Simon Fernandes the winner.

SIMON FERNANDES celebrates. He grabs JACOB.

SIMON: I am king of this school. You are a beggar.

Day fades to night.

OLDER JACOB: I learned something that day, apart from potent effect the memory of the tiger's piss can have on the limbs, I learned something about my nation, about how it works. And as for the Tiger, why that very night …

The sound of boy screaming as he is dragged by the TIGER.

OLDER JACOB: The boy had been playing at the edge of the compound, when he was dragged into the undergrowth. Locals believed the beast was possessed. Many a time wayfarers spoke of an amber light emanating through those trees. So, no one would go to see what remained of the poor boy dragged by the Tiger-Ghoul. Not even the Vicar. Only Fr. Alvares.

FR. ALVARES emerges from the bloody thicket, disheveled. He kneels and prays over the body of the mauled boy, while JACOB and others try to get a glimpse of the corpse.

FR. ALVARES : Don't look boys. Don't look.

OLDER JACOB: In the morning, my Latin tuition continued

Night turns to day.

The VICAR sits listening to JACOB recite the Lord's Prayer.

> Et ne nos inducas in tentationem,
> Sed libera nos a malo.
> Amen.

VICAR: Good. Now Hail Mary

JACOB: Hail Mary, Full of grace
                    The Lord is …

VICAR: In Latin.

JACOB: In Latin?

Beat.

JACOB: I don't know it your Grace. We never studied it.

VICAR: How many times have you heard me say it in church?

JACOB is silent.

VICAR: Were you listening or were you sleeping?

JACOB: Listening your Grace.

VICAR: Then begin 'Ave Maria'

Beat.

JACOB: Ave Maria

Beat.

JACOB: Ave Maria
                         Ave Maria

VICAR: So, you can win races?

The VICAR takes off his belt.

JACOB: Ave Maria
                         Full of graci-a
                         The lord is with thee-a

VICAR: You can win races, but you cannot learn your Latin prayers?

The VICAR hits JACOB with the belt. JACOB howls.

JACOB: Ave Maria

                         Ave Maria

The VICAR whacks JACOB several times with the belt …

VICAR: Learn your prayers boy! Learn your place!

The VICAR is now in a frenzy unable to stop whipping the boy.

JACOB: *(Howling echo.)* Please! Please! Please! Please! Please!

ALAN watches with difficulty. He turns and enters.

AUNT'S APARTMENT. MUMBAI. PRESENT

Everyone laughing. ALAN and DANIEL drinking coffee. In the next room the TV is on.

ALICE: Every day I am drinking coffee.

ALAN: Good!

ALICE: Normally I don't drink coffee, but since I got the nespresso I am drinking coffee everyday … I'm going to watch my programme – leave you two cousin brothers.

She goes.

Beat.

DANIEL: So?

ALAN: So?

DANIEL: After a long time …

ALAN: Yes.

DANIEL: Hotel nice?

ALAN: Can't complain.

Beat.

ALAN: How are you?

DANIEL: Fine. Tickety boo.

They laugh.

ALICE: *(From other room.)* My heart aches. Ask him to find a wife.

DANIEL: *(To ALICE.)* Aren't you watching your programme?

Beat.

DANIEL: So …why are you here?

ALAN: Work – it's been back and forth for a year now.

DANIEL: One year?

ALAN: Yeah.

DANIEL: And only now you come to see us?

ALAN: It's busy, you know. Work, work work.

DANIEL: Hanh.

ALAN: You're busy too with your NGO, I hear.

DANIEL: Hanh.

ALAN: You'll end up winning a Nobel Prize.

DANIEL: You want something?

ALAN: No, I'm fine.

DANIEL: It's funny seeing you after so many years

ALAN: *(Taking out Dad's book.)* Your Mum gave me this.

DANIEL: Read it?

ALAN: I didn't even know he wrote

DANIEL: It was his hobby.

ALAN: He never wrote at home.

DANIEL: Here he had peace.

ALAN: I should give you this *(The book.)*

DANIEL: Why?

ALAN: If it's the only copy /

DANIEL: It's dedicated to you.

ALAN: God knows why. We hadn't spoken. We didn't get on.

DANIEL: Perhaps you didn't know him.

Beat.

DANIEL: He used to sit in that room all day, all night writing. I used to proof read. Sometimes he'd sit so long he'd get cramp. I'd massage his legs and feet. Are you disgusted? I know in UK it's different. Yaw'l want to forget your old folks. Here it's not like that. That's why he came. Why stay there? Who did he have?

Beat.

ALAN: Your Mum wants me to find you a girl

DANIEL: She shouldn't worry.

ALAN: She's just being a Mum.

DANIEL: And how is your marriage?

ALAN: Fifteen years.

DANIEL: Uncle used to tell us your wife was not well.

ALAN: Yeah?

DANIEL: Didn't she try to kill herself once?

Beat.

ALAN: What else did he say?

DANIEL: Nothing.

Beat.

DANIEL: You like this coffee?

ALAN: Does the job.

DANIEL: Nespresso right? We have two of these machines in the office. George Clooney advertises and yet to me it tastes like piss.

ALAN stands.

DANIEL: Going?

ALAN: I have to. Sorry.

DANIEL: Did you ever read my letter?

Beat.

ALAN is about to leave when he spots the watch DANIEL is wearing …

ALAN: Your watch.

DANIEL: What?

ALAN: Where did you get it?

DANIEL: This old thing.

ALAN: That was my watch.

DANIEL: What are you talking about?

ALAN: My bionic watch

19SEVEN9. BOMBAY

ALAN and DANIEL aged seven and eight.

DANIEL: Can I have it?

ALAN: No.

DANIEL: Please

ALAN: It's my watch.

DANIEL: Please. You have so many things.

ALAN: No.

DANIEL: Please I am asking as your best friend, your cousin brother.

ALAN: No.

DANIEL: We can't get anything like this in India.

ALAN: It's my watch.

DANIEL: I'll wear it remembering you. I'll be proud wearing it.

ALAN: You have your things. I have mine.

DANIEL: Please give me. Give it! Give!

PRESENT

ALAN: He crushed it. I remember him crushing it and you crying, your Mum crying, then he took a belt to me.

DANIEL: I don't remember.

ALAN: I do.

DANIEL: He knew how much you had. How much I had. What's eating you Alan? Upset you got thrashed a few times for being a naughty boy?

ALAN: I'll leave this here *(The book.)*

DANIEL: No.

ALAN: You have it. You obviously got on.

DANIEL: You think a dying man hasn't got things to think about? Right till his last day he was writing and he was asking for you. So, take the book. Do what you want with it. Throw it out the fucking window if you want, but take it. It's yours. It's dedicated to you.

ALAN takes the book and leaves.

THE CAR. MUMBAI. PRESENT

ALAN is on his mobile. Outside the Ganapathy celebrations are going on.

ALAN: … In the car … IN THE CAR …There a festival going on …THERE IS A FESTIVAL … I'm not shouting …*(To GHALIB.)* Do you know another way? Hello?

GHALIB does not respond.

ALAN: No not you *(Back on phone.)* … Look I just wanted to say hello … What do you mean why? … I wanted to … Yes, I'm fine … I just wanted to say hello… Okay, okay, bye.

Beat.

ALAN: Are you married driver?

GHALIB: Thirty-three years.

ALAN: That's good.

GHALIB: She dead.

ALAN picks up the book and starts to read.

OLDER JACOB: In life there are things we desire and there are ways and means of getting them. Always we must know what we desire. We must hold it in the mind. My chief job was kitchen boy – food server. In which role, I felt my own hunger keenly, but not for the gruel the cook slopped out. Sometimes hunger causes visions of the mind …

THE KITCHEN

JACOB is transfixed as the veiled MRS PEREIRA approaches him Madonna-like, celestial radiance streaming to the strains of 'Ave Maria'. He kneels in supplication.

The music stops abruptly.

MRS PEREIRA: Give me lunch

JACOB: Yes, Ma'am. Sorry Ma'am. I hope you enjoy it Ma'am.

Given what was on offer, she looks at him strangely.

JACOB: Ma'am?

MRS PEREIRA: Yes?

JACOB: You teach English?

MRS PEREIRA: Correct.

JACOB: I have composed a poem in English. May I repeat it?

MRS PEREIRA: My lunch is getting cold.

Beat.

MRS PEREIRA: Quick.

JACOB: I wandered lonely as a cloud
That floats on high o'er vales and hills
When all at once I saw a crowd
A host, of golden daffodils

MRS PEREIRA: This is Wordsworth only!

JACOB: But, they were nothing to my eye
For beyond them I did spy
More soft than breeze, more pure than air
A heavenly queen, and one so rare
And rarer than the finest jewel,
That sits on top of the King's crown
The koh-i-noor of our dear school
More welcome than when Monsoon rain falls down

And clears the air, bring plants to life
In all the years of my poor life
I will never know anyone dearer or fairer
Than the one we call Mrs Pereira.

Beat.

MRS PEREIRA: What is your name?

JACOB: Jacob, Ma'am.

MRS PEREIRA: Why you are not in my class?

JACOB: The Vicar said I must do my chores before I can attend class.

MRS PEREIRA: I will talk to him.

JACOB: You will?

She goes. JACOB sighs. The COOK and DRIED FISH SELLER look on.

COOK: She is no saint.

JACOB: She is more saint than you will ever be.

COOK: *(Laughing.)* Think so? He thinks she is a saint.

DRIED FISH SELLER: Holy Saint! Virgin!

The DRIED FISH SELLER laughs his dirty laugh.

JACOB: What are you laughing at?

COOK: Nothing.

DRIED FISH SELLER: Nothing. Nothing.

They laugh their dirty laugh again.

JACOB: She is going to ask the Vicar if I can attend her class.

COOK: Is she?

DRIED FISH SELLER: She will beg. Go down on her knees.

They laugh their dirty laughs again.

JACOB: What are you laughing at?

COOK: Nothing. Nothing.

The COOK and DRIED FISH SELLER laugh and laugh …

OLDER JACOB: ENOUGH! I had had enough of this harpy insinuating others were sinners when she was the biggest sinner of all. Call me what you want! Dunk my head in the latrine bucket if you will, but lay one filthy finger on my heavenly Queen …

THE PROVISIONS CUPBOARD. NIGHT

JACOB is saying his Latin prayers. The COOK and DRIED FISH SELLER are outside playing cards and drinking as usual.

OLDER JACOB: That night I said my Latin prayers as usual.

COOK: *(Knocking on the door.)* Open!

JACOB opens the door, looking innocent. The COOK collects coconut oil for her hair.

OLDER JACOB: But, what was I praying for – the deliverance of my soul or for the cook to not notice that I had swapped the coconut oil for herring oil?

The COOK retires to a private place and enjoys the ritual of oiling her hair.

Morning arrives.

The COOK runs into the compound holding her head.

COOK: Ahhhhhh!

JACOB and the boys gather around her.

COOK: Who has done this to me?!

JACOB: What's that smell?

JACOB continues laughing. Hearing this the COOK twigs and chases him round the compound. He runs for dear life.

OLDER JACOB: This time not even the memory of tiger's piss could save me.

The COOK catches JACOB, and wrestles him to the floor. She slaps and punches him several times.

JACOB: It was a joke! It was a joke!

SIMON FERNANDES and other boys gather round and laugh.

The COOK lost in rage finds a massive cooking vessel (a hundi) and bashes JACOB on the head. JACOB collapses.

SIMON: She's going to kill him!

FR. ALVARES seizes her hand before she can hit JACOB again.

COOK: What?! This bastard disgraced me!

ALVARES resolutely holds on.

COOK: Who are you to judge me? At least I don't pretend to be something I'm not.

Think you're better than me? Liars! Drunks! Perverts! I've seen it all here in this shit-stinking latrine. I am good woman. Clean. Enough! I've had enough! *(At some point during this speech the COOK leaves.)*

ALVARES carries the unconscious badly beaten JACOB to a bed.

OLDER JACOB: I was taken to the boy's dormitory. A Village doctor was called.

PANDIT: If he survives the night, he will live, but I do not think he will survive.

FR. ALVARES now prays at JACOB's bedside.

ALVARES: Pater Noster, qui es in caelis,
Sanctificetur nomen tuum.
Adveniat regnum tuum,
Fiat voluntas tua,
Sicut in caelo, et in terra.

Angels arrive. There is a tug of war over JACOB's body: ALVARES vs. the Angels.

  Panem nostrum quotidianum da nobis …
Et dimitte nobis debita nostra,
Sicut et nos dimittimus debitoribus nostris.
Et ne nos inducas in tentationem,

OLDER JACOB: It was said that several times God requested my eternal soul, but each time the ghostly father interceded on my behalf

There is a tug of war continues.

Sed libera nos a malo

Amen.

The Angels relent.

JACOB opens his eyes.

OLDER JACOB: But the biggest miracle of all was that I finally had my desire – a place in the boy's dormitory and in the school.

HOTEL ROOM. MUMBAI

Knocking.

HANNA is in the room. She has a bruise on her face.

HANNA: You're making a mistake Al.

ALAN: What happened to your face?

HANNA: They might be cheaper in Manila, but do you realise what they'll sound like on the phone?

ALAN: What happened?

HANNA: Remember that time I called you about the photocopier?

ALAN: What happened?

HANNA: Felt stupid – each word like a great big sign.

ALAN: Hanna /

HANNA: I kept all your voicemails. Our universe, our secret world. Did you keep mine?

Beat.

ALAN: It's business Hanna. It's change.

HANNA: Do you think you're better than us Al? Driving in your big car yaar? Hiring firing. Giving your driver money for KFC?

ALAN: Has he been talking to you?

HANNA: Big rich English Indian. Did Daddy give you money?

ALAN: Daddy gave me nothing.

HANNA: What do you know about nothing?

ALAN: I started with nothing / I have done this on my own.

HANNA: What do you know about nothing?

ALAN: What happened to your face Hanna?

HANNA: It's nothing.

ALAN: It's not nothing.

HANNA: What do you know about nothing?

ALAN: Hanna /

HANNA: Maybe I slipped. Maybe I had a fight. Maybe I'm not Hanna

ALAN: What?

HANNA: Maybe I'm from a place you can't imagine. No a/c. Just darkness. Maybe my mother was a domestic servant. Maybe one day she just fell dead on the floor. Maybe I stepped over her dead body to reach the light. There are ways in India to reach the light: educate yourself, read books, 'Personal Development' classes, do whatever you have to do to reach the light, the paradise – meeting rooms, offices – you can get there if you believe, if you close your eyes and wish, but maybe it's still there that darkness. Maybe, though I struggle, though I repeat my affirmations, it's still maybe … he's still there …

ALAN: Who?

HANNA: Maybe I told him I was leaving. Maybe he smashed my phone into my face.

ALAN: Who is this man?

HANNA: Do you remember that time I called you about the photocopier?

ALAN: Hanna /

HANNA: Do you keep my messages Al?

ALAN: It's business. It's business.

HANNA: What do you know about business?

ALAN: It's about what you want, what you desire from the core of your being.

HANNA: What do you desire Al? Of what do you dream?

ALAN: Of Manila, of the growth potential there.

HANNA: Maybe I dream of leafy streets, Oxford Street, cosy pubs, Buckingham Palace, Hyde Park in the Autumn just like you told me …

ALAN: If we can get into that market early /

HANNA: I dream of London Eye, Houses of Parliament, Westminster Abbey, The Shard, Westfield Shopping Centre, Hampton Court, the park where you go jogging just like you told me …

ALAN: Maybe you took that a little too seriously?

HANNA: Am I nothing to you?

ALAN: This man – you can't let him do this to you Hanna.

HANNA: What do you care?

ALAN: Of course I care.

HANNA: Take me to London.

ALAN: I'm sorry … I can't …

HANNA: Am I nothing to you?

ALAN: If things were different … it's business Hanna. It's business.

HANNA: Look out the window. Mumbai's a building site no? We have a one hundred thousand new millionaires, our economic growth is eight percent. That's business Al.

She opens the window. Amidst the street sounds – car horns, building works, a beat has started up: A Ganapathy Parade. The drums and the chant 'Ganapathy Bappa Morrya!' build over the rest of the scene.

HANNA: Listen. They're praying to Ganesh – he's the remover of obstacles, and that's the sound of dreams. Millions and millions of dreams – doesn't it excite you? Doesn't it make you hard?

The drumming and parade builds in intensity.

HANNA: It's here Al. Your business. Our dream. I'm the best offer you will ever get. Take it! Take this once in a lifetime offer. It's the real thing. Take it! Feel it! Love it! Fuck it! Take it! Take it!

He embraces her. They kiss.

THE JUNGLE. MANGALORE. 1940

OLDER JACOB: One day Father Alvares took me walking in the jungle.

FR. ALVARES trudges through the undergrowth, rosary in hand. JACOB follows being carrying his violin.

OLDER JACOB: It had long been custom to seek solace in the wilderness. As we strode, I could hear him chanting the rosary for he was a devotee of Our Lady

FR. ALVARES:	Ave Maria

Gratia plena

Dominus tecum

Benedicta tu in mulieribus

Et benedictus fructus ventris tui, Iesus.

Sancta Maria,

Mater Dei,

Ora pro nobis peccatoribus,

Nunc, et in hora mortis nostrae.

Amen.

OLDER JACOB: *(Over the prayer.)* After the space of nearly two hours, we came upon a clearing on the edge of a Mangrove swamp

FR. ALVARES and JACOB sit in the centre of the clearing.

OLDER JACOB: I do not know how long we sat, but there in that stillness, it seemed time itself had ceased.

FR. ALVARES takes out his violin and plays 'Ave Maria'.

OLDER JACOB: *(Over the song.)* Dusk came. Day turned to night … the stars came out smiling. I could see everywhere, everything – the leaves on the trees, the long grass in the breeze, the stalked deer hiding. I was the deer. I was the scorpion in the dust, the scuttling beetle. I was dust, mud, earth, air, the moisture in the air, a molecule, an atom … and suddenly we were floating … rushing, brushing, gushing … this silence was screaming, it is pounding, it is blood curdling, higher and higher we twirl into the night sky… Kings, higher than Kings, shooting stars, gravity nothing, gravity shit, I shit on gravity, I piss on atoms – faster, faster we go, then swoop through the jungle in a swirl, faster than sound, lightning fast, faster than lightning, then in flash back to the clearing … and suddenly it was there … behind us, above us, around us … waiting, watching, breathing … from where has it come? … behind the trees, watching … behind the cool night breeze … waiting, watching, breathing, waiting, watching, breathing …

JACOB: Lost. In the excitement I have lost my father. I search. I hear a sound. I scramble towards it through the tangled trees and there … and there …

From between the trees JACOB spies MRS PEREIRA and the VICAR rolling in a carnal embrace.

I ran into the jungle – faster than my legs would go. I ran till I could run no more. Until eventually, collapsed against a tree, I was exhausted, alone.

Exhausted, JACOB collapses against a tree.

JACOB: Pater Noster, qui es in caelis,
                         Sanctificetur nomen tuum.
                         Adveniat regnum tuum
                         Fiat voluntas tua,
                         Sicut in caelo, et in terra.
                         Panem nostrum …

Sleepy now.

                         Et dimitte nobis debita nostra,

Really sleepy now.

> Et dimitte nobis debita nostra

Head nodding now.

> Et dimitte nobis debita nostra
> Et dimitte nobis …

In Mumbai, in the present there is a knock at the door.

From outside the Ganapathy Parade strikes up again – it builds through the rest of the scene.

ALAN: (*Still reading.*) Hang on!

OLDER JACOB: How long I slept I do not know.

Another knock on the hotel bedroom door.

ALAN: Bloody hell!

OLDER JACOB: But, when I awoke …

Another knock on the door – more insistent.

ALAN: *(Still engrossed)* Hang on!

OLDER JACOB: But, when I awoke …

LITTLE JACOB opens his eyes. A TIGER is fixing him with its gaze.

Another knock at the door.

The TIGER snarls.

Another knock at the door. ALAN gets up still reading the book and answers the door. It is GHALIB, shaken, upset.

GHALIB: Sir.

ALAN: What is it?

GHALIB: It's Ms. Hanna, Sir. It's …

ALAN: What?

GHALIB: She hurt. She hospital.

ALAN: What?

GHALIB: Hit by car. You come. You must come.

Beat.

ALAN: No.

GHALIB: Sir?

ALAN: If you hear anything let me know

The Ganapathy drums and chant crescendo. The TIGER *roars at* LITTLE JACOB.

ACT TWO

THE SCHOOL. MANGALORE

An upbeat Konkani number – maybe 'How Great Thou Art' sung in Konkani, but fast paced, harmony, techno even!

Eight year old JACOB running transforms into fifteen year old JACOB running.

OLDER JACOB: Seven years have passed Alan and here I am, still alive, despite my tangle with the Tiger. The beast simply withdrew. Perhaps it was just not hungry for a little Catholic boy. Anyway, here I am aged fifteen, racing Simon Fernandes again. Of course there were other runners, but by now we were leagues ahead of the pack.

THE SCHOOL. MANGALORE. 1945

JACOB and SIMON, both fifteen years old, are competing against each other again in a long distance race.

SIMON: Nine times nine

JACOB: Eighty-one … nine times ninety-nine

SIMON: Eight hundred and ninety-nine… nine times nine hundred and ninety-nine

JACOB: Eight thousand, nine hundred and ninety-nine

JACOB takes the lead.

SIMON: Henry VIII wives?

JACOB: Catherine of Aragon, Anne Boleyn, Jane Seymour, Anne of Cleves, Catherine Howard, Catherine Parr.

SIMON: I wondered lonely as a cloud

JACOB: That floats on high oe'r vales and hills

SIMON: When all at once I saw a crowd,

JACOB: A host, of golden daffodils.

SIMON: Beside the lake, beneath the trees,

JACOB: Fluttering and dancing in the breeze

    SIMON takes the lead.

SIMON: Largest countries?

JACOB: Land mass? Population?

SIMON: Land mass.

JACOB: Russia, Canada.

SIMON: Population?

JACOB: China … India!

SIMON: Mughal emperors. Babur!

JACOB: Died in the Garden. Hamayun!

SIMON: Died falling down the steps. Akbar!

JACOB: Introduced weights and measures. Jahangir!

SIMON: Let the British in on some good deals. Shah Jahan!

JACOB: Taj Mahal. Aurangzeb!

SIMON: Forbade music. Forbade painting. Forbade everything.

JACOB: Next?

SIMON: What next?

JACOB: After the Mughals?

SIMON: After the Mughals – the British.

JACOB: After the British?

SIMON: After the British?

JACOB: Next? Next?

OLDER JACOB: It was in the air, Alan: The Quit India Movement – the whispering wind brought news of Gandhiji and Nehru – their exploits, their courageous stand against the mighty British Empire. Some of us petitioned the Vicar.

VICAR: *(Reading a pre-prepared statement.)* Though we do not share their extreme political views, we admire their pluck and courage, and wish them well in their attainments. As for us Catholics, there will be no public statements. No shows of support on either side.

CONFESSION:

JACOB: Bless me Father for I have sinned.

FR. ALVARES : What is your sin my son?

The TIGER appears snarling behind JACOB …

JACOB: I feel angry all the time.

FR. ALVARES : Why?

JACOB: I do not know.

Beat.

JACOB: Because people sin and they persist in sinning, while telling others not to sin.

FR. ALVARES : You mean the British?

Beat.

JACOB: Yes.

OLDER JACOB: Actually I meant Mrs Pereira and the Vicar … or did I?

FR. ALVARES: We are all sinners, Jacob. Every one.

JACOB: You are not Father.

FR. ALVARES: Even I … even St Peter – remember how he cut the ear off the Roman Centurion?

JACOB: But, he was protecting Jesus.

FR. ALVARES: So, why was it a sin?

JACOB: I don't know, Father.

FR. ALVARES: Maybe he used an inferior weapon, when a superior one was to hand.

JACOB: What weapon?

FR. ALVARES: Tell me Jacob, what is the strongest weapon of them all?

JACOB cannot fathom.

FR. ALVARES: Begins with 'L'

JACOB: I don't know Father.

FR. ALVARES: Love.

JACOB: Love?

FR. ALVARES: Love is of the soul. Can swords harm the soul?

JACOB thinks.

FR. ALVARES : Love your *enemies* Jacob, is that not what he taught us?

JACOB is silent.

FR. ALVARES : And ask yourself: What is this anger? Where is it coming from?

JACOB is silent.

The HOSTESS sets up a table for the next scene and serves them tea.

RESTAURANT. MUMBAI. MEMBERS ENCLOSURE.

Afternoon. ALAN and DANIEL are drinking tea. The HOSTESS is present.

ALAN: I have fifteen minutes

DANIEL: Talk fast …

ALAN: You wanted to see me.

DANIEL: I wanted? / You wanted …

ALAN: Your Mum called me / said you wanted …

DANIEL: She called me.

Beat.

DANIEL: Bitch.

ALAN winces.

The HOSTESS approaches.

DANIEL: Are you okay?

ALAN: Nothing. Tired.

HOSTESS: Your tea, sir.

DANIEL: How much is a room in this place?

ALAN: I have no idea.

DANIEL: All that money and you didn't sleep?

ALAN: I'm fine.

DANIEL: How much is this cup of tea?

ALAN: What am I, the waiter?

DANIEL: No. You're Richard Branson. Except this is the fifth business you started right? After the other four went bust?

ALAN: Did he tell you that?

DANIEL: After you came crying to him for money?

ALAN stands abruptly.

ALAN: I need the bathroom.

He leaves.

1980

DANIEL and ALAN are now aged eight and nine.

ALAN: *(Over-pronouncing the word.)* Cup of tea old chap?

DANIEL: *(As before.)* Would you like a cup of tea, old chap?

ALAN: That's it.

DANIEL: I sound English?

ALAN: Yeah.

DANIEL: Like a real English gent?

ALAN: No.

DANIEL: A cup of tea, old chap? A cup of piss, old chap?

They laugh.

DANIEL: Shall I piss on you old chap?

ALAN: *(Laughing.)* Er … you homo!

DANIEL: Ha! Ha! I piss on you old chap!

They laugh and fight.

DANIEL: Yaw'l are flying home to London tonight.

ALAN: You'll come to London.

DANIEL: How?

ALAN: In an aeroplane idiot!

DANIEL: We can afford aeroplane tickets idiot?!

ALAN: We'll send you tickets idiot.

DANIEL: Really?

ALAN: Yes, and I'll write.

DANIEL: Really?

ALAN: Three times a year. I'll tell you everything – all my secrets.

ALAN: What?

DANIEL: Sometimes there are things you cannot tell no?

ALAN goes to DANIEL, but he moves away.

ALAN: What?

DANIEL still won't look at him.

ALAN: Tell me.

He wants to say something.

DANIEL: I'll write it in a letter.

Beat.

DANIEL: You will never come back to India, will you?

ALAN: I will.

DANIEL: You won't. I know you won't.

ALAN: I will. I promise. I will.

ALAN hugs DANIEL.

PRESENT

ALAN comes out of the bathroom. He looks ill.

DANIEL: Did you read my letter?

ALAN: I've not got time for this.

DANIEL: Good. *(He stands.)* You won't see me again

ALAN: You bet. I'm off to Manila. Goodbye Mumbai.

DANIEL: Manila?

ALAN: Moving with the times.

DANIEL: Good.

ALAN: And it wasn't four businesses that went bust, it was three and I did go to him for money once, and he didn't give me any. He told me I was useless, pointless. So I sold my car, my flat, but here I am …

DANIEL: A success.

ALAN: You have a problem with that?

DANIEL: What does it mean to you sitting here in an air-conditioned bubble with the windows blacked out

ALAN: Business too tough for you, was it?

DANIEL: We used to have caste in India. Now we have money to make us equal – What equal? It just creates 'us' in the a/c and 'them' out there under the baking sun

ALAN: Go join them Gandhi

DANIEL: I will.

ALAN: They love the malls you know. They 're mad for them.

DANIEL: You think money is the answer?

ALAN: It costs a lot, you know, that cup of tea.

DANIEL: I'm sure.

ALAN: Just like your education costed, the flat you guys live in costed …

DANIEL: Sorry?

ALAN: No wonder you took care of him.

DANIEL: You think it was about money?

ALAN: I remember the old place. The stench.

DANIEL: *(Taking out money from his wallet.)* Here / take

ALAN: You made me shit in the bath because you didn't want me to see the communal toilets, but once I did see them, remember you took me? I could not believe the filth / you people lived in

DANIEL: *(Screams.)* Did you want us to build a palace for you to shit in?

The HOSTESS hovers. Remembering where they are, they both smile at her.

DANIEL: I used to idolize you like some Prince, some Rajah. My cousin-brother from London I used to boast. Now, I realise I should have pitied you because you had money, you had things, but you had nothing

ALAN: I had a toilet.

DANIEL: Enjoy your world-class restaurant Alan, serving pan-Asian fusion cuisine – And you too sick to eat it. You don't know who you are.

ALAN: And you do?

DANIEL: Yes.

ALAN: Maybe you should tell your Mum then.

Beat.

DANIEL: You didn't know your own father, Alan.

ALAN: And you did / I suppose?

DANIEL: You didn't know what he felt / what was in his heart

ALAN: And you did?

DANIEL: Yes.

ALAN: Then you should have been his son.

DANIEL: He wished I was.

ALAN: He should have dedicated that fucking book to you

DANIEL: He wanted to. I told him not to.

ALAN: Why? Why?

Beat.

DANIEL: I have to go to.

DANIEL takes out to pay.

DANIEL: How much is the bill?

ALAN: I don't want your money

DANIEL dumps some notes on the table.

DANIEL: I don't want your debt.

DANIEL is about to go.

DANIEL: You didn't know him Alan.

DANIEL goes. ALAN grabs his stomach, winces.

THE CHAPEL. MANGALORE. 1945

A sermon.

FR. ALVARES : Love your enemies. Do good to them who hate you. Bless them who curse you and pray for them, who despitefully use you. And unto him that smites you on the cheek, offer also the other cheek.

THE JUNGLE. NIGHT

OLDER JACOB: I convened a meeting in the dead of night and there amidst the jungle hush, a rapt crowd of boys heard my voice ring out for freedom.

JACOB addresses the boys.

JACOB: *(As if on a microphone.)* Ours is not a drive for power, but purely a non-violent fight for India's Independence!

FX The sound of a crowd cheering and applauding wildly.

OLDER JACOB: Okay it wasn't like that. Just I and two others, Salvador Saldana and Matthew Rodrigues, not the sharpest tool in the box as they say …

IN THE JUNGLE

SALVADOR: My father says the Brits will never leave

JACOB: I have not yet convened the meeting.

SALVADOR: But, it's just three of us

JACOB: I am the chairman. You are the secretary. The chairman convenes the meeting. The secretary takes notes. I declare this meeting open. Present are chairman Jacob Lobo, Salvador Saldana and Matthew Rodrigues …

MATTHEW puts his hand up.

JACOB: What?

MATTHEW: What am I?

JACOB: You are an ordinary member?

MATTHEW: Ordinary?

JACOB: Yes.

MATTHEW: I want a title.

JACOB: Shut up!

SALVADOR: Proposition: The Brits will never leave India.

JACOB: The British will leave. We will make them leave.

SALVADOR: How? By non-violence?

JACOB: Exactly.

SALVADOR: What about Subhas Chandra Bose – he says we should fight, become soldiers /

JACOB: We are soldiers. Non-violent soldiers.

MATTHEW: If I was in a war and saw a non-violent soldier, I'd just kick him in the balls or shoot him in the head *(He play-acts what he would do.)* then stab him then punch him then shoot him then stab him /

JACOB: Ahimsa!

MATTHEW: Bless you.

SALVADOR: 'Ahimsa' means Gandhiji's philosophy of non-violence.

MATTHEW: Oh!

JACOB: Ghandiji has said: 'non-violence is not a cover for cowardice, but it is the supreme virtue of the brave … It is a conscious, deliberate restraint put upon one's desire for vengeance.'

SALVADOR: We want vengeance against these bastard Brits.

JACOB: Ghandiji has said 'if we were to drive out the English with the weapons with which they enslaved us, our slavery would still be with us even when they have gone'.

SALVADOR: Then, how to drive the English out?

JACOB: With the strongest weapon …

The other boys puzzle.

JACOB: Begins with 'L'

MATTHEW: Lathi canes?

JACOB and SALVADOR look at him.

JACOB: Love.

SALVADOR: Love? Love is a weapon?

The boys ponder. SIMON now steps into the clearing.

SIMON: Point of order Mr Chairman.

JACOB: You.

SIMON: The British have been fair to us you think these Hindus and Muslims will be the same?

JACOB: Of course they will.

SIMON: *(Laughing.)* You see if they come to power, how much they will love us Catholics.

JACOB: Gandhiji said: 'the reins of power may be handed to some others whose names are not heard in the Congress today'

SIMON: Gandhiji has said, Gandhiji has said, we all know what Gandhiji has said. What we don't know is what his Hindu and Muslim friends will do, should they come to power.

JACOB: The Mahatma is a pure soul. He would never /

SIMON: Pure … *(Sniggers.)*

JACOB: … What?

SIMON: I heard he is queer soul, a difficult old man – violent to his sons

JACOB: Rubbish. *(To SALVADOR.)* Scrub that from the minutes Mr Secretary.

SIMON: Furthermore, my father's friend knows someone who stayed in his ashram – says he sleeps next to a naked girl at night.

MATTHEW: Why?

SIMON: To test his purity.

SALVADOR: *(Laughing.)* I'd like to test my purity like that.

SIMON and SALVADOR laugh.

SALVADOR: Sometimes I'd fail the test, but what the hell!

They laugh.

SALVADOR: Some you win. Some you lose.

They laugh.

SALVADOR: I'd be a good loser!

They laugh.

JACOB: *(To SALVADOR.)* Scrub that from the minutes this minute!

SIMON: Gandhi's a dirty old goat!

MATTHEW now does an impression of a lecherous goat…

SIMON: So, how can you trust his word?

MATTHEW continues with his goat impression. SALVADOR joins in …

JACOB: Gandhiji is the light. Ahimsa is the way.

SALVADOR laughs and continues with his goat impression.

SIMON: Proposition: A vote of 'No confidence in the chairman'.

JACOB: Impossible.

SIMON: I propose that I be chairman.

JACOB: No.

SIMON: All those in favour say *(Mimicking a goat.)* 'Aye'

SALVADOR / MICHAEL: *(Goat enthused.)* Aye. Aye.

JACOB: Cancel that from the minutes.

SIMON: Okay. My first act as chairman is to declare that Jacob Lobo is a beggar, a plate cleaner. My second act is to declare Ghandiji's dirty old goat.

SALVADOR / MATTHEW: *(Goat Sounds.)* Aye. Aye

SIMON smiles at JACOB in triumph.

OLDER JACOB: As he smiled I heard him say it.

SIMON: I am king of the class Lobo. You are beggar.

JACOB attacks SIMON, who fights back. JACOB gets the upper hand. SIMON struggles. JACOB pushes his face hard into the dirt.

SIMON: What about non-violence?

JACOB pushes SIMON's face harder into the red dirt. MATTHEW panics and runs off.

SALVADOR: Salvador Saldhana – apologies for early absence.

SIMON: Please!

SALVADOR runs off.

SIMON: You're hurting me! Please!

JACOB pushes SIMON's face into the dirt.

SIMON: Please! Please! Please! Please! Please!

An amber light through the trees. The TIGER emerges snarling.

JACOB lets go of SIMON.

It is clear that only JACOB can see the TIGER.

Upset SIMON runs away…

The TIGER approaches JACOB…

It now pins him against a tree, snarling like it did at the end of Act One…

JACOB opens his eyes. The TIGER walks away.

The TIGER turns round and looks at JACOB almost coyly.

A seductive drumbeat starts …

JACOB follows the TIGER.

The TIGER *takes off his* TIGER *mask, beneath which it is an androgynous God – wild, suggestive, sexual.*

Drums and music. (some of the words may be spoken – to unsettling effect – as in a Kurt Weill number)

TIGER SONG *(Upbeat.)*

Life is short and full of steam
You're a loose twig in the stream
Believe not everything that seems

You are small and full of fear
I could eat you, leave one ear
But, I won't cos I want you near me

If you want to know what's real
Look inside yourself and feel
All the fears, all the joys
All the girls and all the boys
They're the same thing in the end
In a life that never ends

When you've lived ten thousand lives
You had husbands you've had wives
You just give off fancy vibes like moi

Show me what you have inside
What you are and what you hide
So I can atleast decide whether to eat you

Thought abandon, now be free
Follow me into the trees
Through the jungle of your soul
Through your deepest, darkest hole
In the mangroves of your mind
Just what secrets will you find?
Just what secrets will you find?

APARTMENT. MUMBAI. PRESENT

An Indian soap opera is on the TV – it's soundtrack intense, melodramatic.

ALAN is on the sofa, looking quite ill now.

ALICE: Arre idiot! Nimbu pani.

ALAN: No.

ALICE: Lemon water, baba!

ALAN: I can't hold it down Auntie

ALICE: What have you eaten? / Something from the street?

ALAN: Nothing. No.

ALICE: Then?

ALAN: I was in the restaurant yesterday. I suddenly felt something cold in my stomach.

ALICE: It's your anger.

ALAN: No /

ALICE: Your anger has done this to you.

ALAN: I've ingested bacteria – that's all.

ALICE: You're angry Alan.

In the next room the TV drama crescendos, it is intense.

ALAN: Can we turn that down please?

ALICE: It's my programme.

ALAN: *(Sharp.)* Turn it off.

She goes next door and turns the TV off. He gets the book, when she comes back – he has put it on the table.

ALICE: Kya? (What?)

ALAN: It's the book / you gave me.

ALICE: I know what it is idiot

ALAN: Take it

ALICE: It's yours.

ALAN: Just take it.

ALICE: No.

ALAN hurls the book out the window …

ALICE: Arre!

A clatter, a cry, a dog barking several stories below.

ALICE and ALAN go to the window.

ALICE: Idiot!

Somebody shouting up in Hindi: 'Are you trying to kill me?'.

Beat.

ALAN: I'm going.

ALICE: Where?

ALAN: Manila. Take care of yourself – use that coffee machine.

ALICE: Your Daddy loved you.

ALAN: You can make cappucino, frappucino, Americano,

ALICE: He was proud of you / Everyday he told us how proud of you he was.

ALAN: filter coffee, Latte, mocha… there's a booklet.

ALICE: Your own company, beautiful wife.

ALAN winces as his stomach grumbles.

ALICE: Talk to Daniel.

ALAN laughs.

ALICE: Who will you know in India after I'm gone?

ALAN: I'm not from here. I don't speak the lingo. I can't eat the food. I get a lung infection if I breathe the air. It's up my nose, in my lungs, in my brain.

ALICE: Why didn't you read his letter?

ALAN: I can't remember.

ALICE: You promised. When you promise, you don't forget.

ALAN: I have to run

ALICE: Why did you come? To give me that book? You could have put it in a bin at the airport.

ALAN: They don't have bins in airports anymore.

ALICE: There is nothing more important than family.

ALAN: What did family ever do for me? Beat me up! Criticise? Fuck family! Indian families most of all. It's lies. All lies. Just like that book. There weren't even tigers in Mangalore in the 1940s. I googled it. I googled 'Tigers in Mangalore'. It's lies. All lies.

ALICE: No.

ALAN: Okay let's talk about why Daniel's not married.

She now goes into the kitchen.

ALAN: Why is it the guy's nearly forty and never had a girlfriend?

ALICE: Go!

ALAN: I thought you wanted me to /

She comes back.

ALICE: He needed you. He wrote to you. Say it again 'I can't remember. I can't remember'. I can and I'm the one with the memory problems, but you can't remember. Then forget. Forget!

ALAN: Auntie /

ALICE: Go. Take your coffee machine. I don't drink coffee. I remember that now I hate it. It makes me sick.

She goes into the kitchen.

ALICE: Take it to London, or Vanilla or wherever. Take your Vanilla coffee machine and go.

She comes in with (a part of) the machine. She throws it on the ground.

But, AUNTIE in a rage is destroying the coffee machine.

ALAN leaves.

He walks into the street right into the heart of the Ganapathy Parade: dancing, drumming, colour, riot.

An effigy of Ganesh bears down on him.

The Street. Mumbai / The Jungle. Mangalore.

In the Mumbai street the chaos continues.

The following NARRATOR lines can be divided up between all the company as dancers / revellers in the Parade.

OLDER JACOB: I followed the Tiger into the jungle.

ALAN is shocked.

NARRATOR: Think you can throw me out of the window?

ALAN walks on …

NARRATOR: Deeper we went in leaps and bounds.

The NARRATOR pursues ALAN.

NARRATOR: You're useless! You're pointless!

ALAN tries to get away.

NARRATOR: You can't even hear my story as it's meant to be.

ALAN covers his ears.

NARRATOR: Listen. Listen.

ALAN closes his eyes.

NARRATOR *(All)* Listen!

The TIGER roars at ALAN and at JACOB. ALAN uncovers eyes and ears startled.

TIGER: Come with me …

OLDER JACOB: Into the mists he led me, in the midst of the mists, into an open space where the everything was dancing … everyone … men dancing with men, women dancing with men, women dancing with women … the trees, the sun … dancing

The beat is strong now, seductive, Indian-infused techno.

We watch the VICAR and MRS PEREIRA getting sexy.

Men dancing with men, women dancing with women.

ALAN turns – he is in the Mumbai Street. A man is trying to get him to dance.

DRUNK MAN: Dance with me! Dance!

ALAN: Fuck off!

DRUNK MAN: Where you from?

ALAN tries to get away.

DRUNK MAN: You like dancing! This is real Bombay dancing!

ALAN pushes him away. Turns again.

He is back in the jungle: JACOB and the TIGER.

OLDER JACOB: Further into the mists … he drew me …

The music and dance beat goes softer now …

OLDER JACOB: Listen to how my story should sound.

TIGER: *(In Konkani.)* What have you done since I last saw you?

OLDER JACOB: *(Translating.)* What have you done since I last saw you?

JACOB: *(In Konkani.)* Many things

OLDER JACOB: Many things. *(To ALAN.)* You're lost in translation boy.

TIGER: *(In Konkani.)* What have you done?

OLDER JACOB: *(Translating.)* What have you done?

JACOB: *(Konkani.)* I have worked hard in studies and in sports

OLDER JACOB: I have worked hard in studies and in sports.

The TIGER roars. It is terrifying. JACOB and ALAN cower. Older JACOB laughs.

JACOB: (Konkani.) What do you want?

OLDER JACOB: *(Translating.)* What do you want?

TIGER: *(Konkani.)* What do *you* want?

OLDER JACOB: *(Translating.)* What do *you* want?

JACOB: *(Konkani.)* To do well in studies and in sports.

OLDER JACOB: *(Translating.)* To do well in studies and in sports.

TIGER: *(Konkani.)* What do you desire?

OLDER JACOB: *(Translating.)* What do you desire? *(To ALAN.)* Listen … listen

TIGER: *(Konkani.)* Of what do you dream?

OLDER JACOB: *(Translating.)* Of what do you dream?

JACOB: Of London!

TIGER: *(Konkani.)* Of whom do you dream?

OLDER JACOB: Of whom do you dream?

JACOB: *(Konkani.)* Nothing. No one.

OLDER JACOB: *(Translating.)* Nothing. No one.

TIGER: *(English.)* What do you desire? Who do you desire?

OLDER JACOB: *(English.)* I closed my eyes as it led me further through the mists and there in the mists, in the midst of the murky mists …

The drums have by now faded out to permit perfect stillness.

The mists clear to reveal:

FR. ALVARES plays 'Ave Maria' on his violin. YOUNG JACOB watches enraptured …

OLDER JACOB: *(Over the music.)* It was the most beautiful … the purest, most exquisite … and in its melody I felt … It plays in my mind, I am a little boy standing in adoring silence of his Father … his dearest, kindest … what was that silence? I cannot … some things cannot … You showed me wonders. The trees alive with spirits … wonders have no rules. What rules? … I must let go. I can't, after all these years I can't. Though I've tried, but still you come to me … and sitting here to this very day I'm broken. I did not believe in magic, but it exists … what one soul feels for another is magic … it is pure … it is not wrong … it is not wrong …
it is not wrong.

The PRIEST stops playing and looks into JACOB's eyes.

The TIGER roars.

JACOB: *(Roaring.)* No!

JACOB roars like the TIGER. In some sense he is now the TIGER.

FR. ALVARES : Jacob? Jacob!

JACOB pushes the priest.

OLDER JACOB: I pushed him. I pushed him into the mire.

The PRIEST falls.

THE GANAPATHY PARADE. MUMBAI

The 'eye' of the Ganapathy parade has moved past ALAN, but there is still noise and chaos in the air.

HANNA: Hey Al! Got your call. The photocopying. Doing it now. They say 'Best time of day is now' … Great (She laughs) enjoy Sunny London. Greetings from Mumbai, where it's raining actually. *(She laughs.)*

He presses 'Play'.

HANNA: Hey Al! Got your call. The photocopying. Doing it now. They say 'Best time of day is now' … Great *(She laughs.)* enjoy Sunny London. Greetings from Mumbai, where it's raining actually. (She laughs)

He presses 'Play' in his head.

HANNA: Hey Al! Got your call. The photocopying. Doing it now. They say 'Best time of day is now' … Great *(She laughs.)*

He presses play in his head.

HANNA: Hey Al … Enjoy … London *(She laughs.)*

Play.

HANNA: Hey Al! … Enjoy … now *(She laughs.)*

Play.

HANNA: Hey Al! … Enjoy … now *(She laughs.)*

Play.

HANNA: Hey Al! … Enjoy … now *(She laughs.)*

Play.

HANNA: Hey!

ALAN reaches for HANNA who fades. He collapses onto the floor. GHALIB finds him in the crowd

GHALIB: Sir? Come!

ALAN: I can't.

GHALIB: Too much people.

ALAN: Are you trying to cheat me?

GHALIB: No, Sir /

ALAN: I need to go to Manila

GHALIB: I take you hotel Sir.

ALAN: AIRPORT!

GHALIB: Don't shout at me Sir.

ALAN: TAKE ME TO THE AIRPORT.

GHALIB: Don't shout at Ghalib.

ALAN: I'M THE BOSS.

GHALIB: You sick Sir?

ALAN: I'M THE BOSS

ALAN faints.

JUNGLE. MANGALORE. 1945

JACOB holds FR. ALVARES who is sinking into quicksand.

JACOB: Hold on! Father! Hold on!

FR. ALVARES : Let me sink. It is what I deserve.

JACOB: No, Father you do not deserve.

FR. ALVARES : Let me sink Jacob.

JACOB: No!

FR. ALVARES : Always I was nothing. Dirt.

JACOB: You are not dirt. You are my Father.

FR. ALVARES : I am a sinner.

JACOB: No, father!

FR. ALVARES : Always I have been a sinner.

JACOB: No!

FR. ALVARES : Let me sink Jacob. Let me go!

JACOB: You are my Father! You are my Father! FATHER!

The PRIEST sinks below the quick sand.

SLUM / CHAWL. MUMBAI. PRESENT

The stage is bare and dark.

ALAN is weak – standing before him, a dark figure, a man, played by the same actor who plays GHALIB.

ALAN: Ghalib?

MAN is silent.

ALAN: What happened?

MAN is silent.

ALAN: Where is this place?

MAN is silent.

ALAN: Ghalib!

MAN remains silent.

ALAN: Christ's sake!

MAN remains silent.

ALAN: It stinks in here. This country stinks. I need to get to Manila.

Beat.

MAN: You don't like India Sir?

ALAN: What?

MAN: Why are you here?

ALAN: Online clothing retail …

Beat.

MAN: I used to wear good clothes when I was young. I used to dance.

ALAN: Did you?

MAN: You like dancing Sir?

ALAN: No.

> *The MAN clicks – Bollywood music plays loudly – played earlier in the restaurant with HANNA.*

MAN: Dance!

ALAN: Turn it off! Turn it off!

MAN: This is film music sir. You like films?

ALAN: Turn it fucking off!

MAN: There is one film sir - a man has a daughter and he loves her more than anything. But, another man comes and uses her badly and the Father, you know what he does Sir? You know what he does?

> *The MAN 'clicks' the music off.*

MAN: What films you seen Sir?

ALAN: I saw this one with my cousin once.

MAN: Name?

ALAN: I can't remember now

MAN: Name!

ALAN: It was a James Bond thing … Agent 116.

MAN: I'm Agent 116 and you are the Bad Boss.

ALAN: No I'm Agent 116

MAN: They danced in that film Sir?

ALAN: Yes. *(He laughs.)* James Bond was dancing.

MAN: Show me Sir.

> *The MAN clicks again and the music comes on – loud and speeded up.*

ALAN: Turn it off!

> *The MAN clicks again the music is even faster, even louder. ALAN covers his ears. The MAN 'clicks' the music off.*

ALAN: Do you want money? Is that what this is?

MAN: How much you got sir?

ALAN: In my wallet … /

MAN: Ten crore? Twenty crore?

ALAN: I don't know.

MAN: You know how much I got? You know how much I got?

    The MAN laughs.

ALAN: Who are you?

    The MAN laughs.

MAN: I am God. I am the Father.

ALAN: I am your boss.

MAN: Dance boss.

ALAN: No.

MAN: Dance!

ALAN: *(Alan grabs the man.)* No!

MAN: Take your dirty hands off me!

    The MAN pushes ALAN across the space.

ALAN: That's it. That's you.

MAN: You want soda? Coca cola?

ALAN: Not the guy you present in the book

MAN: You have everything you need Sir?

ALAN: You beat me up.

MAN: I win!

ALAN: But, I'm a success.

MAN: You think life is grand hotels, Sir?

ALAN: I was happy when you died.

MAN: You want KFC?

ALAN: I thought it was my fault, but it was you. It was all you.

MAN: I'll take you to hospital, Sir to see my girl

ALAN: Your girl?

MAN: I'll take you to hospital to see my daughter Sir.

ALAN: She's your … she's your …

MAN: Do you pray Sir?

ALAN: What?

MAN: Are you not afraid of the dark Sir?

The MAN clicks. Darkness.

ALAN: Ghalib! Stop it! Stop it!

A terrifying sound: The roar of one billion, two hundred fifty-two million Indians.

The lights back on. ALAN is kneeling.

MAN: Pray.

ALAN: I didn't know she was your daughter.

MAN: Say your prayers.

ALAN: I don't know any prayers …

MAN: Pray

ALAN: Our Father,
Who art in heaven
Hallowed … Hallowed be thy name …
Thy Kingdom come
Thy will be done
On Earth … on Earth as it is …

The MAN goes off to get something. A gun? A knife? He returns and watches ALAN.

        Give us this day our daily bread
And forgive us our trespasses
As we forgive those …

The MAN watches ALAN.

ALAN: As we forgive those …
As we forgive those …
As we forgive …

ALAN stands. The MAN stands.

The face each other for several moments.

Blackout.

Distant drums. ALICE comes in.

ALICE: Ready?

ALAN: Do those drums never stop?

ALICE: Drums?

ALAN: The Ganapathy drums … dum dum durum dum.

ALICE: That is the aircon.

   Beat.

ALAN: How did I get here?

ALICE: Your driver brought you

ALAN: I was in a room with a man /

ALICE: Your driver.

ALAN: I was in a room.

   Beat.

ALICE: So, you are going to Vanilla?

ALAN: Home.

ALICE: Where the heart is.

ALAN: I'm leaving my wife.

ALICE: Oh dear.

ALAN: We don't like each other.

ALICE: Oh dear.

ALAN: I met someone.

ALICE: Who?

ALAN: Doesn't matter.

ALICE: I met someone – Bal Raj – you threw the book hit the poor fellow on the head *(She gives him the book which has been sello-taped.)* Thirteen stories it fell

   She gives him back the book.

ALICE: Let's call Daniel.

ALAN: No.

ALICE: You were friends.

ALAN: It's broken.

ALICE: Fix it.

ALAN: Don't keep asking him to marry.

ALICE: Why?

ALAN: You know why Auntie.

An SMS.

ALICE: Time.

ALAN: I'll see you.

ALICE: No.

ALAN: I'll come back.

ALICE: Next time I will be up. UP!

ALAN: No.

ALICE: Yes.

Beat.

ALAN: And the coffee machine. I'll send another

ALICE: I had it fixed.

ALAN: How?

ALICE: You can fix anything in India idiot.

THE TAXI. PRESENT

ALAN: Ghalib

GHALIB is silent.

ALAN: What happened?

GHALIB is silent.

ALAN: In that hut … in that room?

GHALIB: You fever.

ALAN: You talked to me. You told me /

GHALIB: No sir. Dream. Just dream.

Pause.

ALAN: She's your daughter, isn't she?

GHALIB is silent.

ALAN: How is she?

GHALIB does not respond.

ALAN: I want to see her.

GHALIB does not respond.

ALAN: Turn the car round.

GHALIB does not respond.

ALAN: Turn it round, Ghalib!

GHALIB: She not want to see you sir. Leave her. Leave.

ALAN is silent. He picks up the book.

THE TRAIN. MANGALORE 1947

OLDER JACOB: And so, Alan my story nears it end. A year since Fr. Alvares was swallowed by the mire. Word arrives the Indian Air Force is looking for a new fighter pilot and every respectable school is to select three students to attend a day of testing and interviews in Bombay.

A train whistles.

OLDER JACOB: Here we are on the train home.

The train chugs away.

SALVADOR and SIMON are quiet. JACOB is inconsolable.

JACOB: Idiot!

SIMON: Who are you calling idiot?

But, JACOB was referring to himself.

SALVADOR: Jacob man! Don't feel bad. You know how it works in India. It was probably given to some politician's son. It's not for the likes of us. We're not going to get in an airplane and fly across the sea.

JACOB: I reached for it. I reached.

SIMON: Too high!

JACOB: One day I'll get it. I'll fly

SIMON: In what?

Beat.

SALVADOR: Where will you fly Jacob?

JACOB: Away.

The sound of an aeroplane taking off.

OLDER JACOB: I can see it now a mango in the tree.
You remember Alan, right at the start, right at the start,
right at the start. Walking with my brother I saw it.
I reached for it. I reached …

DEPARTURES. MUMBAI. PRESENT

ALAN reads. Next to him a young girl is listening to music on headphones.
The music is loud and can be heard through the headphones.

ALAN: Can you turn that down please?

INDIAN GIRL: Ha?

ALAN: Your music.

INDIAN GIRL: It's a free world, mister.

ALAN: Can I be free of your music?

INDIAN GIRL: Are you unhappy?

ALAN: Just turn your music down

INDIAN GIRL: Where are you flying to?

ALAN: London.

INDIAN GIRL: That explains it.

ALAN: Where are you from?

INDIAN GIRL: Mumbai.

ALAN: Greatest city in the world

INDIAN GIRL: Why not?

ALAN: Ask the beggars.

INDIAN GIRL: We haven't got there yet, but we're getting there.

ALAN: Just turn your music down.

INDIAN GIRL: We do what you do better, cheaper. We're dreaming. We're coming up.

ALAN: What?

Beat.

INDIAN GIRL: You look unhappy dude. Do something about your life.

ALAN: I'll remember that.

ANNOUNCEMENT: Flight A1603 to New York now ready to board.

She gets her stuff together and is about to go.

ALAN: What's your number?

INDIAN GIRL: Why do you want my number?

ALAN: If you're ever in London…

INDIAN GIRL: I could be your daughter dude.

She is about to go.

INDIAN GIRL: Listen

She puts her headphone on him.

ALAN: What is it?

INDIAN GIRL: The future.

We hear what ALAN hears 'Indian Infused Techno' maybe the same we heard as TIGER led JACOB through the Jungle – the sound of India remaking itself, new dreams.

She goes, but something of the music stays.

OLDER JACOB: And so, Alan, one story remains…

ANNOUNCEMENT: Flight BA203 to London Heathrow now ready to board.

OLDER JACOB: I reached for it. I reached.

ALAN makes a call.

DANIEL's phone rings. He ignores it.

The phone continues ringing.

ALAN gets ready to board the plane.

The phone rings and rings …

ANNOUNCEMENT: Last call for Flight BA203 to London Heathrow.

OLDER JACOB: I reached …

ALAN walks off.

The phone rings and rings. DANIEL ignores it.

OLDER JACOB: Reach.

The phone rings.

ALAN: It's me. It's Alan. I did read your letter.

Pause.

ALAN: Hello?

A plane takes off. A tiger roars.

Blackout.